D0249513

ACCIDENTS IN NORTH AMERICAN MOUNTAINEERING

VOLUME 10 • NUMBER 2 • ISSUE 65

2012

the
**AMERICAN
ALPINE club**
WHERE CLIMBERS UNITE

THE AMERICAN ALPINE CLUB
GOLDEN, CO

THE ALPINE CLUB OF CANADA
BANFF, ALBERTA

© 2012 The American Alpine Club

ISSN: 0065-082X
ISBN: 978-1-933056-77-7
ISBN: (e-book) 978-1-933056-78-4

Manufactured in the United States

Published by:
The American Alpine Club
710 Tenth Street, Suite 100
Golden, CO 80401
www.americanalpineclub.org

Cover Illustrations

Front: An exuberant Jimmie Dunn demonstrates the spacious nature of the "Corkscrew Summit" of Ancient Arts in the Fisher Towers near Moab, Utah, on an early free ascent. Photo: AAC member *Bob Palais*

Back: Dave Weber, paramedic and High Mountain Ranger of Denali NPS, performs a training exercise with pilot Andy Hermansky in June 2011. Worldwide, short-haul missions are becoming a more popular method to retrieve injured climbers from higher altitude. Three weeks prior to this training, Andy performed the highest short-haul rescue in North American history. (See AK, May 12.) The peak in the background is Mount Foraker. Photo: AAC member *Menno Boermans*

♻ Printed on recycled paper

CONTENTS

WARNING! The activities described within Accidents in North American Mountaineering (ANAM)—including but not limited to: rock climbing, ice climbing, mountaineering, backcountry skiing, or any other outdoor activity—carry a significant risk of personal injury or death. The owners, staff, contributors, and volunteers that create this publication recommend that you DO NOT participate in these activities unless you are an expert, have sought or obtained qualified professional instruction or guidance, are knowledgeable about the risks involved, and are willing to assume personal responsibility for all the risks associated with these activities. ANAM and its publisher, the American Alpine Club, MAKE NO WARRANTIES, EXPRESSED OR IMPLIED, OF ANY KIND REGARDING THE CONTENTS OF THIS PUBLICATION, AND EXPRESSLY DISCLAIM ANY WARRANTY REGARDING THE ACCURACY OR RELIABILITY OF INFORMATION CONTAINED HEREIN. The American Alpine Club further disclaims any responsibility for injuries or death incurred by any person engaging in these activities. Use the information contained in this publication at your own risk and do not depend on the information contained herein for personal safety or for determining whether to attempt any climb, route, or activity described herein. The examples/ stories contained herein are anecdotal and/or informational only and not intended to represent advice, recommendations, or commentary on appropriate conduct, standards or choices that you, the reader, may make regarding your own activities.

SAFETY ADVISORY COUNCIL 2012
The American Alpine Club
Aram Attarian, John Dill, Chris Harder, Daryl Miller (ret.), Jeff Sheetz, and John E. (Jed) Williamson (Chair)

MANAGING EDITOR
John E. (Jed) Williamson

ASSOCIATE EDITOR
Aram Attarian

COPY EDITORS
Gwen Cameron, Joe Forrester, Erik Hansen

KNOW THE ROPES CONTRIBUTORS
Rob Hess, Rick Weber (graphics)

LAYOUT
Dan Gambino

ADDITIONAL THANKS
Erik Lambert, Janet Miller, Meredith Milnes, Emma Walker

ACCIDENTS IN
NORTH AMERICAN MOUNTAINEERING
Sixty-fifth Annual Report of The American Alpine Club

This is the sixty-fifth issue of Accidents in North American Mountaineering.

Canada: Data and narratives not available from 2011. Visit alpineclubofcanada.ca/services/safety/index.html for information on the Alpine Club of Canada's safety program.

United States: We have created a new section in ANAM called "Know the Ropes: Fundamentals to Save Your Life" that will target common causes of many of the incidents analyzed herein. We hope this will increase awareness and education and thus help prevent incidents. The topic for this year is rappelling, which seems especially appropriate given that since 2000, there have been 74 reported errors in this category. This year alone there were 12 incidents, nearly double the average.

We are grateful to Rob Hess for writing this section and to Rick Weber for turning Rob's images into the illustrations.

We have not included Mountain Rescue Units in the U.S., primarily because their Web site contains this and much more information. We encourage you to visit their Web site: www.mra.org.

Aram Attarian has become associate editor as a result of his narratives and data collection from the Southeast and Colorado. In addition to the AAC professional staff, Erik Hansen and Joe Forrester continue their volunteer contributions as copy editors.

Along with the dedicated individuals on the Safety Advisory Council, we are grateful to the NPS rangers who forward their incident reports and to all individuals who send in or post their personal stories.

We lost George Sainsbury, our loyal and faithful reporter from the Northwest for many decades. A special thanks to his wife, Mary Lou, who is continuing the tradition by sending along clippings from that region.

John E. (Jed) Williamson
Managing Editor
7 River Ridge Road
jedwmsn@mac.com

Know the Ropes: Rappelling

Fundamentals to Save Your Life

By Rob Hess, UIAGM/IFMGA

Graphics by Rick Weber

The annual report Accidents in North America Mountaineering (ANAM) has been the definitive source of information regarding incidents occurring in the climbing and mountaineering community on a yearly basis since 1950. The careful analysis of such incidents is vital to the identification of common mistakes made by climbers and what might have been done to mitigate them. Very few incidents occur that are what one might call "acts of nature". Human error is the overwhelming cause of all incidents. Even in cases where these "acts of nature" occurred, one can often trace the chain of events back to some form of error in judgment on the part of individuals involved, ultimately allowing them to be vulnerable to such natural hazards.

For the 2012 edition, Know the Ropes focuses on rappelling. We will first look at the common causes for rappelling incidents and then provide best practices for addressing them.

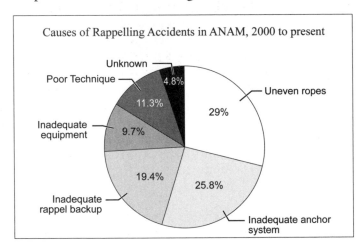

Causes of Rappelling Accidents in ANAM, 2000 to present

A review of the primary causes of rappelling incidents from the year 2000 to the present reveals:

1- Inadequate anchor systems, or in other words, anchor failure.
2- Inadequate back up for rappels.
3- Rappelling off the end of the rope(s)—largely due to uneven ropes.

Less common causes include:
1- Rappel device issues.
2- Stranded due to inadequate rappel rope length.
3- Harness/belay loop failure.

Plan ahead!

The first step in avoiding any climbing incidents is good prior planning. Get all the information you can from the guidebooks. It is also a good idea to take a copy of a route topo—even if you have done the route before. And consider looking at blogs and talking with friends or acquaintances for information.

Equipment inspection before each season—and before each climb—is always important. Is it time to retire your ropes, slings, or harness? Look closely at all the gear to see if there are any obvious wear and tear issues and consult the manufacturers for recommendations.

1. Anchoring Systems

What about anchor construction and/or inspection for descending? If you climb in popular areas on popular routes, you might expect that descent routes will be well established. But what if you get off route? What if there is severe weather? What if you need to bail? It is not a bad idea to carry a couple of 7mm by 5-meter cords on multi-pitch routes. They function well to tie together multiple points of protection for anchors on the ascent and can be very useful for building or enhancing anchors on descent. Consider a couple of double slings or what might be referred to as four-footers. It is not a bad idea to carry a small safety kit: bail carabiner with a dedicated auto block sling, knife, 5/16" quick link, and even a Tibloc or similar small ascending device.

- Assessing Fixed Anchors:

If using pre-slung objects, be sure to inspect slings thoroughly. Often the slings go behind fixed objects and are not readily visible, so be sure you see that all portions of the slings are in good condition and have not been compromised by little creatures or weathering action. If slung around natural objects such as boulders or trees, be sure to test the objects for security. How big is the tree? Normally it should be at least six inches in diameter and well rooted. How big and secure is the boulder? Get behind it and test it by pushing on it with your legs. Also be sure the anchor sling won't slip off the back.

Are there any metal descending rings or has the rope been running directly on the sling material? If the latter, it could result in damaging the sling upon rope retrieval. If in question, add a sling and add a 5/16" quick link, which has a working load of 1720 lbs. and a breaking strength 5280 lbs.—or bail carabiner wherever possible. The quick links are preferable because they are easily found at hardware stores

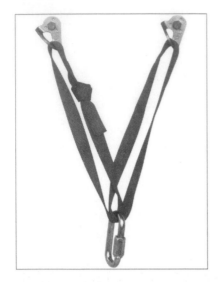

Figure 1

and inexpensive; and since they have a screw gate, they are easily added to existing anchors.

- Building and Configuring Anchors:
Climbers need to have a working knowledge of bolts (including what modern bolts look like) and to understand what to be suspicious of. In general, bolts are considered to be solid pro. When you know the protection points are good, in this case the bolts, one sling tied in the "magic X" configuration, otherwise known as self-equalizing, is useful in that it uses minimal sling but equalizes the pull on the protection points. The drawback is that it reduces the redundancy of two bolts down to one sling, and should one point pull out, the system will be shock-loaded. In all anchoring cases consider a quick link. (*See Figure 1.*) If tattered slings are already attached to fixed anchors, consider removing them, which is one reason to carry a pocketknife.

• If building and slinging an anchor for descent, do not skimp on protection. Isn't it better to leave a bit more personal gear rather than face the consequences of the anchor failing? When looking for your anchor point, consider the available protection and also consider the position of the rope and whether it will pull effectively and/or come off cleanly without knocking off rocks. Clearly the protection must be good, for if it is not, nothing else matters. When slinging the protection there are several ways to entrain all points. Regardless of how you construct the anchor, consider equalizing all points such that they share the load equally. Also consider rigging the anchor so that the system is redundant. Then, if a protection point were to fail, the system would not be shock-loaded. (*See Figures 2 & 3.*)

2. Rope Rigging and Management on Descents

Proper rigging and rope management is integral to proper risk management on descents. With a bit of pre-planning and preparation, common incidents that occur during descents can be avoided.

- Rigging Ropes:

Whether using one rope or two for descents, ensuring the ropes are equal in length is important to avoid one of the most common mistakes.

Figure 2

Figure 3

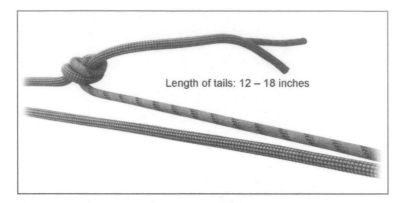

Figure 4

• If using a single rope, is there a middle mark on the rope? If so, and more importantly, is this mark accurate? (E.g. the rope may have been cut.) If working with a rope where the middle mark is not obvious, thread the end of one rope through the rappel anchor and then match both ends. Then while pulling the rope through the anchor, keep both strands together as you stack the rope until no rope is left. The bite in the anchor is the middle point. Temporarily tie an overhand knot in the bite—above the anchor—so when the rope is thrown off, the middle is not accidently lost.

• If working with two different ropes, ask yourself if the ropes are equal in length. It is not uncommon to have ropes from different manufacturers that are said to be the same length but turn out to be quite different in length. Measure ropes in relation to each other before getting into a sticky position.

• A good knot to use to tie two ropes together is the flat overhand. This knot has been called a number of things and has at times been unfairly demonized. When used correctly, this knot is superior. Its advantages are that no matter what orientation it starts in, when it comes time to pull the ropes, the knot shifts into an advantageous position that avoids getting caught up or stuck. Simply be sure the knot is well dressed, very snug and has a minimum of 12 inches of tail on both strands. (*See Figure 4.*)

- Knotting, Throwing and Descending Ropes:

Once the ropes are in the anchor, consider temporarily tying the ropes off to the anchor before throwing them so you do not lose where they are positioned. Also, there is no reason to rappel without the ends of the rope secured in some way. A few questions to ask:

• Have you tied knots in the ends of the ropes to ensure you do not rappel off the ends? Consider tying knots in each individual strand as oppose to tying them together, as this lets kinks dissipate. The triple barrel knot is a good choice. (*See Figure 5.*) In some cases, knotting the ends and throwing the ropes might be a recipe for stuck ropes. This is common in windy conditions or on routes known for the features that like to catch ropes! If this is the case, knotting the rope-ends and then clipping them off to your harness thus allowing control of the ends might be a good choice.

• Throwing ropes requires technique and practice. Again, remember to tie off the rope(s) temporarily before you throw them. One good technique is to butterfly coil the first half of one of the rappel strands, then butterfly the second half of the same strand with the end. Throw the first half off, wait a few seconds, then throw the second half (with the end). Repeat with the other strand.

• Is throwing the ropes the only option? If the weather is windy and/or the trajectory of the ropes is in any way impeded by trees, bushes and other obstacles, you might consider saddle bagging the ropes down the rappel. (*See Figure 6.*) To do this, separate both strands of rappel ropes so the strands are not crossed. Start with the end of one strand, knot the rope, then butterfly the strand starting with large coils progressing to small coils. This will ensure easy feeding of the rope. Use a single or two-foot sling to cradle the coil and clip off to your gear sling on your harness. Do not girth hitch the coil with the sling. Repeat with the other strand of rappel rope.

• What if my rappel does not reach the anchor and I am stranded? There are some important points for this. First, can you build an anchor with the equipment you have where you are? If you are the first person down a rappel, be sure you have the rack with you. Second, if you are unable to build an anchor, do you have the ability to improvise and ascend the double strand back to the rappel anchor or to a point where an anchor can be built? Having an ability to improvise and ascend ropes with slings and cord is an essential skill to have.

3. Rappel Systems and Backups

When ready to rig the rope(s), take a moment to think through the sequence of events to follow. Be sure you have set up different systems for rappels and practice securing yourself to the different anchor systems. Consider taking advantage of a secure location to plan and prepare as much as possible for the descent before getting into an exposed stance. Be sure that you can anchor at the top rappel and all subsequent anchor points. If descending a route with multiple rappels, have an understanding as to how you will you protect yourself and other members of your party.

Figure 5

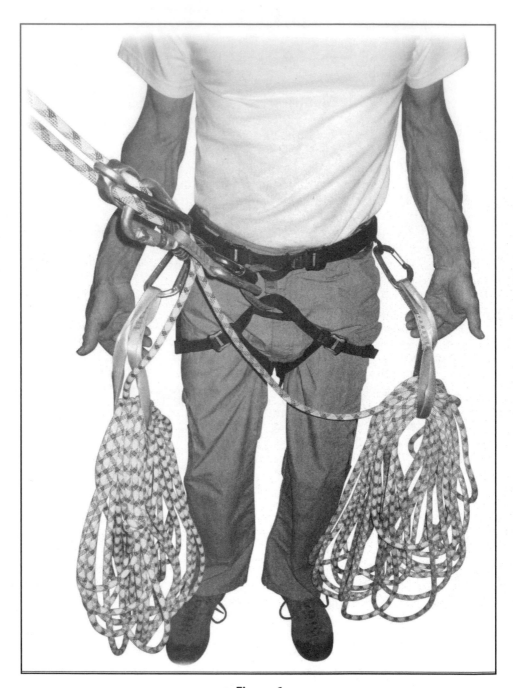

Figure 6

- Rappel Backups:

There are several ways to protect oneself when rappelling. As is evident from the "causes" graph, common issues involve rappelling off the end of the rope due to the rope ends being unequal in length, no knots in the ends of the ropes, or ineffective personal friction hitch rappel backups. Adding a friction hitch to the rappel system is one piece of the puzzle that increases security. It is best done on the brake-hand side of the system, still ensuring a majority of the load in any situation where the backup is employed is on the rappel device. The friction hitch of choice is the auto-block. This hitch has the advantage of being quick to rig, easy to slide down the rope(s) and manage with one hand, and bites well if the hitch is suddenly loaded. The main disadvantage is that unlike other friction hitches, the auto-block can be released or caused to slide under load if it hooks up against or bumps into an object. A common and dangerous example of this is if the auto-block hitch sling is too long and slides up against the rappel device.

Rappel backups allow for what is referred to as "hands free" or "locked off" mode. This allows the rappeller to troubleshoot problems such as stuck or tangled ropes, route cleaning, and items stuck in the rappel system. Rappel backups in the form of an auto-block are really only necessary for the first person on a particular rappel. Subsequent rappellers can be protected by a simple "fireman's belay" from the first person down. In this belay form, the first person down can hold on to the rappel lines and if necessary pull tight on the ropes to arrest any unwanted movement on the part of the rappellers above.

- Rappel Extensions:

When descending, it is necessary to have a rappel device available as well as a sling/tether system to enable clipping in to subsequent rappel anchors.

• The common system of rappelling with the device attached to the belay loop and the back up attached to the leg loop of the harness can be effective, but is hard to adjust so that the auto-block sling does not move up against the belay device, thereby sliding and becoming ineffective. Better ways of rigging rappels so that the auto-block sling does not bump against the rappel device involve rappel device extensions.

• A very important point to note is that all extension systems that attach to the harness via nylon on nylon—such as the four-foot sling or the personal anchoring slings (PAS)—must be girth hitched directly to the tie-in points of the harness. Harness manufacturers specify that slings or personal anchoring slings are not to be girth hitched to the belay loop. When setting up rappel extensions that include tethers for anchoring, some key rigging points are:

• If rigging an extension from a four-foot sling, use nylon slings, not Dyneema. Dyneema has a high strength-to-weight ratio but has very

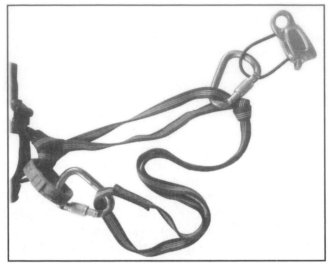

Figure 7

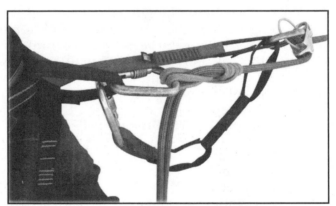

Figure 8

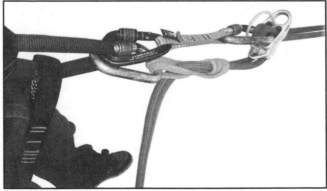

Figure 9

little elasticity, breaking under low loads when shock loaded. (See the study on video by DMM at dmmclimbing.com/video.asp?id=5).

• When using a four-foot sling, first girth hitch the sling to the tie-in points, being sure the sewn portion is positioned out near the end of the sling. Next, tie an overhand knot in the sling at a point roughly less than half the distance to the end of the sling. This will allow you to clip the tether back to the belay loop with a locking carabiner when not in use while still attached to the rope with the rappel device clipped to the sling on the harness side of the overhand knot. (*See Figure 7.*)

• If using a PAS, first girth hitch the PAS to the tie in points. Next, choose a loop to clip your rappel device to that is less than half the distance to the end loop that acts as the clip-in tether. (*See Figure 8.*) This again will allow clipping the tether back to the belay loop with a locking carabiner as discussed above.

• An additional rappel system that is simple and easy to use but does not incorporate an anchoring tether, utilizes a quick draw with two locking 'biners. (*See Figure 9.*)

• One common rappel device problem is when clothing or hair get caught in the rappel system. Pocketknives are of course invaluable, but the rappel extension serves to put the rappel device in a position that mitigates the problem by keeping the device further away from hair and clothing.

• Please also note: Daisy chains are for aid climbing and should not to be used as personal anchoring slings.

Communication and commitment

Table II in ANAM shows that about 30 percent of climbing accidents happen on descent. Clearly the ones that end in fatality or serious injury are a result of rappel errors that are for the most part avoidable.

We have covered the set-up systems that will keep you safe. The other human factors are communication and the importance of remembering that you and your partners are a team, so watch out for each other—stay aware! Check each other and double-check all systems. In terms of communications, if you are unsure of what was said, ask again.

This ending leads us to the Know the Ropes topic for next year: lowering errors, both in terms of systems and communications.

UNITED STATES

ICE AVALANCHE
Alaska, Denali National Park, Moose's Tooth, Root Canal Glacier

On April 24, Ben Kiessel (27), Chris Scharf (38) and Chris Lackey (39) landed on the Root Canal Glacier below the South Face of the Moose's Tooth with the intention of climbing the "Ham and Eggs" route. On April 27, they had climbed up to the eighth pitch and turned around due to thin ice conditions. Upon returning to camp, they met two guides, Kevin Mahoney and Larry Cote, who had set up camp immediately next to theirs.

About 0115 on April 18, the climbers heard the crack of a serac wall collapsing and moments later were engulfed in the blast of an avalanche while in their tents. All five were blown out of their tents and two were partially buried by debris. After he came to a stop, Kiessel took inventory of the scene and said that Mahoney and Cote seemed to be ok. He then found Scharf buried from the waist down and Lackey buried head down with just his feet sticking out of the snow, still in his sleeping bag. They were able to get him out and found him to be breathing, but unresponsive, with blood in his mouth and nose and a "beat up" face. They placed him in sleeping bags with pads on the ground and were able to find a sat phone on which the called NPS for assistance at 0130.

The rescue was not able to launch until 0650. By that time, Lackey had succumbed as a result of traumatic injuries.

Analysis

Ice avalanches (serac falls) result from tensile failure within the ice due to ice flow (creep) within the ice mass and/or glide at the bed surface. It is inherently difficult to predict the timing of this type of failure. Unlike the situation with snow avalanches, there is very little correlation to time of day, aspect, elevation or weather. This leaves few tools available to the practitioner for use in the field. Avoidance and limiting the time of exposure continue to be the best practice. I once overheard a seasoned avalanche professional trying to describe timing of ice avalanches say, "And as for seracs… all I can say is if it looks like it is going to fall it is probably going to fall."

The run-out distance for an avalanche is the farthest point to which debris can reach. Currently, the best methods for determining run-out distance are "…by long-term observations of avalanche deposits; (2) observations of damage to vegetation, ground or structures; or (3) searches of the historical record as preserved in newspapers, old aerial photos, or other written material" (McClung and Schaerer, 2006). Unfortunately very few of these are available for the mountains of the Alaska Range, so we must use other methods.

The debris from this event traveled 1,920 feet out from the point of impact on an average slope angle of six degrees. This is a substantial distance on a shallow slope angle, and thus it retained enough energy to hit the camp with impressive force. Similar to water, the main flow channel followed the path of least resistance. A subtle depression channeled the majority of the debris (up to feet deep) and deposited it directly through the area of the campsite.

Another significant terrain feature that contributed to this event is the nearly vertical avalanche path. The vertical fall of approximately 743 feet allowed for an almost "free fall" environment for the ice to travel, increasing the speed at which it fell. This appears to have created an explosive impact that broke ice into small pieces allowing them to travel greater distances, also resulting in a substantial air blast that traveled in front of the debris. The air blast hit with such force that it ejected all five climbers from their tents, hurling them into the air ahead of the debris, accounting for their position mostly above or shallowly buried in the debris.

The timing of large avalanche events are sometimes described in terms of "100-year events", indicating that events this large only happen once every 100 years much like a 100-year flood. They are in effect rare events. This is a dangerous assumption in this case. The hanging glacier that produced this event is capable of producing a much larger one and this size event seems to happen on a more regular basis. Based on interviews, a Google Earth image that captured a similar debris zone and this event, it appears that the return period for this size event is much more frequent than 100 years. It may have a return period as frequent as every five to ten years or less.

An additional component was the guides' decision to place their camps in this location. Historically, camps on the Root Canal have been used on both sides, up and down the entire airstrip. The approximate campsite location where the accident occurred is a popular area often used by many climbers each year for its view of the entire "Ham and Eggs" climbing route and proximity to plane access. Interviews indicate that there were previous campsites from this season in this location and none in other locations. Choosing camping locations in this area is difficult due to the large scale of terrain and multiple potential hazards (rockfall, snow avalanches, weather, and serac fall) that threaten the basin. At times one may trade one for the other, making decisions difficult, even for experienced guides.

Professionals often rely on experience to help guide their decision making process. However, experience-based decisions are not always flawless. Studies have shown that novices and professionals make decisions using "heuristics" or mental shortcuts (Tremper, 2008). These shortcuts allow for quick decisions during complex tasks and are based on limited information. Two heuristics that professionals are especially prone to are "social proof" and "familiarity" (McCammon, 2002). In this case the existing campsites and historical use of this area may fall into McCammon's "social proof" category. "The social proof heuristic is the tendency to believe that a behavior is correct to the extent that other people are engaged in it" (McCammon, 2002). One of the two guides had also been to the area many times and camped in a similar location on seven previous trips without incident. His decision may fall into the "familiarity" category. "The familiarity heuristic is the tendency to believe that our behavior is correct to the extent that we have done it before" (McCammon, 2002). An additional heuristic that I will add is potentially a calibration problem regarding snow avalanches and ice avalanches resulting from the possible assumption that they behave like the same animal when they do not.

Complex terrain in the Alaska Range demands attention to detail every step of the way, and timing will always be a part of it. Using all of our tools to avoid and reduce exposure will help to reduce the risk but cannot take away all of the risk. The decision to camp in this location worked for many people for many seasons, but not this time. (Source: John Leonard, South District Ranger, and Peter Armington, Investigating Officer.)

(Editor's Note: Request bibliography from Denali National Park.)

FALL ON SNOW, FATIGUE, FROSTBITE, EXPOSURE
Alaska, Denali National Park, Mount McKinley, West Buttress

On May 12, during a Mountain Trip expedition led by guide Dave Staehli (56), Jeremiah O'Sullivan (40) suffered a fall while descending Pig Hill at approximately the 19,700-foot level, below the summit of Denali. During the fall, he broke his leg and others suffered minor injuries. A different client in the same party had descended with another guide earlier in the day due to signs of frostbite. Staehli and two climbers, Beat Niederer (38) and Laurence Cutler (45) left O'Sullivan near the location of the fall and descended towards the high camp at 17,200 feet on the West Buttress route. Along the way the group was separated and Niederer died from exposure. O'Sullivan was rescued via helicopter. Staehli and Cutler were treated for injuries including frostbite at high camp and flown off on subsequent days.

The forecast for this period of days was for high winds and party to mostly cloudy skies, but both groups observed generally good weather and inaccurate forecasts. On May 11, both groups decided to try for the summit. Mountain Trip 2 (MT2) left high camp at 1121 and Alaska Mountaineering School (AMS 1) left at 1145. When MT2 arrived at Denali Pass (18,200 feet), Staehli noticed that climber Tony Diskin had frostbite on two fingers of both hands and sent him back to high camp with guide Henry Munter. Diskin was wearing gloves and a lightly insulated jacket and reported having had cold fingers and toes all morning.

After receiving an initial call for assistance from Patrick Ormand (Alaska Mountaineering School and AMGA Mountain Guide) at the 17,200-foot camp regarding missing clients high on the mountain from another expedition, a major Search and Rescue operation was initiated by South District Ranger John Leonard (IC). Mountaineering rangers Joe Reichert and Coley Gentzel were assigned the Operation Chief and Planning Chief overhead positions, respectively. The Rescue Coordination Center (RCC)—a US Air Force operation —was contacted and additional aviation assets were requested and were able to respond to the incident. Ultimately, late in the day, the NPS contract helicopter was able to evacuate Jeremiah O'Sullivan from the Football Field area near the summit of Denali after the strong winds that had enveloped the peak had subsided.

O'Sullivan's life was most certainly saved through the use of the short-haul technique in what was the highest altitude evacuation using such a method in North America. A short time later Beat Niederer's body was evacuated from the vicinity of Denali Pass, also utilizing the short-haul technique. Sadly, Beat Niederer had succumbed to unknown injuries and/or the extremely adverse weather conditions that were present. On May 13, the two other members of the party who also had significant injuries were evacuated from the mountain, also using the short-haul technique.

Analysis

Extensive interviews of the climbing team members and other teams on the mountain did not bring to light any significant issues or factors contributing to the events leading directly up to accident on the upper mountain. One climber from another team who was interviewed did note that at several points during his multiple interactions with the Mountain Trip team (MT2), led by Staehli, that many members of the group seemed quite fatigued and it did not seem that they were taking care of themselves. This comment was primarily directed at interaction he had with the team at the 16,200-foot level on the West Buttress, and then as his team passed MT2 along the summit ridge. (Source: John Leonard, Mountaineering Range, and Coley Gentzel, Lead Mountaineering Ranger)

(Editor's Note: There were 229 climbers on Denali on May 12, including 67 clients, 36 guides, 114 private climbers, and 12 NPS on patrol. An external investigation team had not completed its report at the time of publication.)

FALL ON SNOW – UNABLE TO SELF-ARREST, CLIMBING UNROPED
Alaska, Mount McKinley, Denali Pass

On the morning of May 16 at 0545, the Angolo Dell' Avventura Expedition team of Luciano Colombo (67), Mauro Colombo, and Paolo Civera left the 17,200-foot camp for a summit attempt. While gearing up to leave, they decided they would not rope up for ascending the Autobahn, but brought their rope in case they felt like they needed it up higher. It took them approximately two and a half hours to climb to Denali Pass, where they took a break for food and water. At this time, the team had a discussion about the weather, which was beginning to get cloudy above Denali Pass. They decided to keep moving up. At Zebra

Rocks, approximately 200 meters above Denali Pass, the team decided to return to the 17,200-foot camp due to clouds and poor visibility. At Denali Pass they regrouped and discussed using their rope for descending to the camp. Paolo Civera and Mauro Colombo tied into the rope for the descent of the Autobahn, but Luciano Colombo felt that the terrain was moderate enough to not tie into the rope. They left Denali Pass together with Civera and Mauro Colombo on the rope ahead of Luciano Colombo (unroped), not separated by more than 30 meters. At approximately 18,000 feet, 50 meters down from Denali Pass on the Autobahn, Civero heard Luciano yelling, "Paolo, Paolo!" Mauro and Paolo turned and saw Luciano in a sliding fall out of control. Civera and Mauro Colombo could only watch as he continued to fall out of sight down towards the Peter's Glacier. He came to a stop at approximately 16,500 feet. The distance of the fall was about 1,400 feet.

Ranger Matt Hendrickson witnessed Luciano Colombo falling the last half of the slope at 0956. Hendrickson called the incident into 14,200-foot camp and advised Ranger Kevin Wright that he would respond to the scene with three VIPs on his patrol and to advise Talkeetna Ranger Station.

Hendrickson arrived on scene at 1110 with VIP Paramedic Richard Alexander. Alexander determined that Luciano Colombo had sustained head injuries during the fall that were incompatible with life and found no vital signs. After packaging Luciano Colombo's body, Hendrickson and three VIPs began moving the body back to the 17,200-foot camp, arriving at 1425. On May 18, Luciano Colombo's body was flown to Talkeetna.

Analysis

Team Angolo Dell' Avventura had spent nine days on Denali, ascending to 17,200-foot camp before their summit attempt on May 16. The team was feeling good, had no notable issues with the altitude, and felt rested the morning of their summit attempt. Time spent reaching Denali Pass was on average and the team made a sound decision to come down due to poor visibility and deteriorating weather conditions. The one major contributing factor in this incident was Luciano Colombo's decision to not tie into the rope with his partners for descending the Autobahn. In this case, an experienced, 67-year-old mountaineer, not taking the consequences of a fall into consideration and not taking simple safety measures of using a rope, was the ultimate cause of his death. (Source: Matt Hendrickson, NPS Mountaineering Ranger)

AVALANCHE – FALL ON SNOW
Alaska, Denali National Park, Mount Frances

On May 23 two Japanese climbers, Jiro Kurihara (33) and Junya Shiraishi (28), were reported a day overdue after they left Denali Base Camp in an attempt to climb Mount Frances a few days prior. NPS rangers took a recon flight around Mount Frances for signs of the climbing party and spotted some dark shapes in what appeared to be avalanche debris at the bottom of a significant gully on the west side of Mount Frances. Upon landing near the location, rangers uncovered the bodies of the two missing climbers and determined that they had been either swept off of the face by an avalanche or had fallen from a point high on their climbing route. Both were deceased and had suffered significant trauma associated with a long fall in complex terrain.

Analysis

The climbers had chosen to climb in a period immediately following new snowfall that totaled somewhere in the neighborhood of 12 inches. The slopes they were climbing on had likely not received much in the way of sun exposure, and a significant warming event following the storm. In observing their chosen route and the point that it seems they fell from, it is hard to tell if their fall triggered a wet snow avalanche, or if perhaps they were swept off the upper portion of their route by such a slide. Regardless, their resting place was at the bottom of a large avalanche gully, and their bodies and equipment were mostly buried by avalanche debris. Perhaps they exercised poor judgment in choosing to travel on loaded slopes during a warm period of the day or perhaps it was just an unfortunate and somewhat random event. (Source: Coley Gentzel, Lead Mountaineering Ranger)

FALL ON SNOW – FAILURE TO CLIP IN TO FIXED ROPE

Alaska, Mount McKinley, Denali Pass

Early in the day on May 25, several groups went for a summit attempt from the 17,200-foot camp. The Alpine Ascents guide stopped by the NPS tent to let Rangers know that they would be attempting to summit.

At 2315, NPS volunteer Mik Jedlicka noticed something below Denali Pass, approximately half a mile from camp. She used a spotting scope to confirm it was a group of four climbers, then heard a shout for help. Based on the location of the group, it was apparent they had fallen from the standard trail on the Autobahn from around 18,400 feet. I notified Ranger Tucker Chenoweth at the 14,200-foot camp, and then quickly went to other tents at the 17,200-foot camp to recruit help. I initially contacted Mountain Trip guides and the Para-rescue/Dutch team (Windmill) with Robert Schnell, Matt Kirby, and Alexander Naumann. Alex Sargent of Team Ranger and NPS volunteers Andrew Dietrick, Mark Dalpes, Mik Jedlicka, and Anthony Larson M.D. were also in the initial rescue party. The hasty teams mobilized quickly with minimal gear set to triage, and the following teams brought more medical and rescue gear including a Cascade toboggan and a Sked litter. Schnell (paramedic) did the initial triage when he arrived at the patients. He prioritized James Mohr (30) as Immediate (difficulty breathing, unconscious, closed head injury), Gary Burke (31) Urgent (lower leg fracture, scalp laceration, head injury, alert and oriented). The other two climbers, Suzanne Allen (41)—a guide for Alpine Ascents—and Peter Bullard (46), had no signs of life and were declared deceased.

Most of the rescue team worked on stabilizing and packaging the two patients while the Mountain Trip guides fixed a guiding line to protect the traversing crevassed terrain back to the 17,200-foot camp. An immediate helicopter evacuation was put on hold until adequate daylight allowed for safe flying conditions. At this point the time was around 0030.

Two independent teams pulled the patients back to camp, one in the Cascade toboggan, one in the Sked litter. As we got close to camp, I radioed to Jay Casello of the Para-rescue team (Windmill) to request additional strength to pull the patients into camp. Numerous other climbers, including the entire Dutch team (Windmill) came out to help.

The patients were placed into two VE-25 Park Service tents which served as dedicated patient treatment tents. Schnell maintained primary care of the critical patient and Larson was the lead provider for the urgent patient. Schnell performed a cricothyrotomy to keep an open airway on the critical patient and continued respirations with a bag-valve mask and supplementary oxygen. Military medics from team Windmill assisted care of both patients under the leadership of Schnell and Larson. Both patients were monitored as the daylight increased.

At 0420 the Park helicopter launched from Talkeetna. Pilot Andy Hermansky flew to 17,200 feet. He picked up the critical patient and returned to Base Camp, then flew to 17,200 feet a third time to pick up the urgent patient and take him to Base Camp as well. Both patients were transferred to LifeMed helicopters and taken to Anchorage hospitals.

Analysis

Some details are missing to thoroughly understand the sequence that took place and caused the fall. Only one member of the team recalls the events, and he suffered some head trauma and memory deficit from the injuries. Based on the survivor's accounts, the guide initially began the traverse descent from Denali Pass as the last person on the rope. This puts the guide above the clients and is the traditional position for a mountain guide on this traverse. As the team moved onto the Autobahn face, the guide noticed that the fixed protection pickets were not being clipped onto the rope by the leading person. She took corrective action and reversed the rope team, putting herself in the lead and in charge of clipping the protection. There may have been a deviation from the standard trail as the team moved onto the traverse due to confusion of the new and old trails. During the course of making this transition or shortly after the guide assumed the lead, a climber fell. At this point no pickets or other protection were clipped to the rope. The first fall was stopped initially, but apparently pulled other climbers off their stances and initiated another fall. Ultimately the sequence of falls led to the entire rope team of four climbers being pulled off the trail and down the slope. The vertical fall distance to the point of rest was estimated at 1,000-1,200 feet. The angle of the slope averaged over 40 degrees, with some areas closer to 50 degrees.

The circumstances that caused this fall are attributed to climbing without adequate protection.

Autobahn history: The location of this incident has historically been the most dangerous section of the West Buttress climbing route. At least 14 climbers have died in falls on the Autobahn and many others have suffered significant injuries from falls down the slope. Most falls happen on descent from a long and tiring summit day when fatigue is most significant. It remains a challenge for mountaineers to negotiate the Autobahn safely, despite the efforts of the National Park Service and guiding companies to keep fixed protection in place to arrest falls. The slope is steep enough to make it very difficult to arrest a fall once initiated, especially in firm snow or icy conditions. Traveling roped together on the Autobahn without protection in place puts the entire team in jeopardy if one climber were to slip. A guide has little chance to arrest the fall of a client without the benefit of snow pickets to absorb the energy of a fall.

Fixed protection: An issue that came up multiple times this season involved groups having their climbing protection or carabiners removed by other teams so that it was not available for the descent. A common tactic is for groups to place carabiners on the 20-24 fixed pickets on the Autobahn and leave them in place for the day, only removing them after they pass by the second time on the descent. If the leader of a rope does not have extra carabiners available and none are with the pickets, then they do not have the means to use the fixed protection. With a client leading a rope team and responsible for assuring that protection is clipped, the guide may not be aware of the type, quality, or absence of protection on the rope. The NPS and guide companies have tried different solutions to keep carabiners fixed to the pickets and they still disappear. We don't know if the guide left carabiners in place and was expecting them to be available for descent, or if her gear may have been removed by other teams, but it is a likely scenario.

Another possible cause of confusion was the presence of two trails on the Autobahn. The older trail used in previous years was not favored or maintained due to an open crevasse midway up the slope. The new trail for 2011 took a higher route than normal and was maintained beginning in early May by the first guided teams. Descending climbers on several occasions this year unintentionally took the lower route, which did not have pickets for protection. The lead climber of the Alpine Ascents rope team may have moved onto this lower trail and found no pickets available.

Debrief point: This was a resource-intensive rescue at high elevation with critically injured patients. A large team of 14 experienced and acclimatized rescuers was instrumental in the favorable outcome of the two survivors. (Source: Kevin Wright, Mountaineering Ranger)

ALTITUDE ILLNESS, EXHAUSTION, CLIMBING ALONE – SEPARATED FROM PARTY
Alaska, Mount McKinley, Denali Pass

On June 6 at 2000, Park Ranger Tucker Chenoweth was descending from 19,500 feet with four volunteers when they observed solo climber Zeljko Dulic (27), of the Expedition Serbia Denali, who appeared to be suffering from an altitude-related illness. Based on a rapid physical exam, Chenoweth decided to have Dulic evacuated.

At 2021 another solo climber, Sho Tamagawa (22) of the Meiji University Expedition 2011, stumbled and fell due to altitude and exhaustion near the location of Dulic. Tucker and his team performed a rapid physical assessment on Tamagawa and the decision was made that he needed to be evacuated as well. Between 2021 and 2043, the two climbers were individually short-hauled in a Screamer Suit using the NPS contract helicopter down to the 14,200-foot camp, loaded internally and transferred to awaiting LifeMed ships at Base Camp. Zeljko Dulic refused further care after being transferred to Life Med.

At 2137, it was reported that another solo climber of the Meiji University Expedition 2011, Masaaki Kobayasi (20) was lying down at 18,700 feet, apparently suffering from altitude illness. After descending to the location and performing a rapid physical exam of the third climber, Chenoweth requested a separate short-haul mission to evacuate this patient, which was done. Chenoweth and his volunteers descended to 17,000 feet without further incident.

Analysis

All of the climbers involved in the rescue were members of larger expeditions. At some point they all separated from their teams and attempted to solo climb the upper mountain. Poor decision-making, altitude sickness, and exhaustion are contributing factors to all three of these incidents. The luck of having the helicopter at Base Camp, ready for short haul as well as having Ranger Chenoweth high on the mountain possibly saved the lives of some of the individuals. (Source: Tucker Chenoweth, Mountaineering Ranger)

ILLNESS – CARDIAC DIFFICULTIES
Alaska, Mount McKinley, West Buttress

On June 7 at 0836, an NPS mountaineering patrol enroute to the high camps encountered a 58 year-old male climber at approximately 7,000 feet on the Kahiltna Glacier experiencing significant chest pain and labored breathing. The patient reported a history of cardiac problems, including a prior heart attack two years ago. The patient denied the current problem was a heart attack, and after an initial examination by NPS medics, declined their recommendation for immediate helicopter evacuation. However, the patient's symptoms and vital signs were consistent with an active cardiac emergency, one which NPS medics felt required immediate, advanced medical intervention. In addition, rapidly deteriorating weather conditions indicated that the window of opportunity for air evacuation was soon to close. The rangers reiterated to the patient their recommendations and concerns, emphasizing the importance of early treatment for potential cardiac emergencies, combined with the threat of incoming weather that could possibly keep the patient on the glacier for several days. The patient consented to evacuation by helicopter and at 1002 was evacuated from the site by a LifeMed B-3 air ambulance helicopter. The patient was transported to Mat-Su Regional Medical Center where he was admitted to the facility's Intensive Care Unit for cardiac evaluation and treatment. (Source: Mark Westman, Mountaineering Ranger)

CARDIAC ARREST
Alaska, Mount McKinley, West Buttress

On June 10, Brian Young (52) went into sudden cardiac arrest in his tent at high camp after having climbed to the summit of Denali earlier that day. The team that he was climbing with reported that during their summit climb, he suffered from altitude illness and was affected to the point of vomiting several times, stumbling, and losing his footing while descending to high camp. Upon his arrival at high camp, his climbing companions suggested that he check in with NPS rangers at high camp, but Young stated that he felt fine and would prefer to take a nap. He entered the tent, which was occupied by two other climbers, and they reported him falling asleep quickly and immediately exhibiting Cheyne-Stokes breathing. Shortly thereafter, they did not hear any breathing sounds coming from his sleeping bag. They opened his bag to find him unresponsive and not breathing. His tent mates notified NPS rangers who initiated CPR, which was terminated after 30 minutes due to no signs of a pulse. After conferring with the NPS medical director, Brian Young was pronounced dead at 1100. Poor weather delayed recovery of his body until June 16.

Analysis

Although it's difficult to predict who might develop an emergency cardiac condition while climbing at high altitude, it stands to reason that individuals with a history of cardiac issues can be considered at higher risk.

According to interviews with family members, Brian Young had no history of cardiac issues; however, he was reported to have lost 30 pounds in the four to six weeks leading up to the start of his climb. Common side effects of rapid weight loss are changes in blood sugar level, changes in blood pressure, electrolyte imbalance, and a higher risk of heart arrhythmias. Brian Young was described by all those who climbed with him on Mount McKinley as strong and healthy, with the exception of those who climbed with him above 17,200 feet. On his summit climb, Young was reported as having bouts of ataxia and vomited several times. Despite suggestions from his summit partners, Young did not feel like he had any reason to seek medical assistance once he was back at the 17,200-foot camp.

Although medical resources are very limited at the high camp, timely medical intervention might have been helpful in averting the final outcome. (Source: Coley Gentzel, Lead Mountaineering Ranger)

(Editor's Note: Episodes of illness, while not technically climbing accidents, are counted and some are reported each year. Some illnesses actually result in such accidents as falls on rock, snow, or ice. Some result in significant rescue efforts that may put park personnel and others at risk. Altitude-related illnesses are often due to rapid ascent and/or age and not being in good physical condition. In the case of guided clients, some have pre-existing conditions that they have not reported, which may include both illnesses injuries that flare up as a result of exercise and/or altitude.)

FALL ON SNOW, CLIMBING ALONE IN SEVERE WEATHER CONDITIONS
Alaska, Mount McKinley, West Buttress

On the evening of June 28, a guided group at high camp radioed NPS rangers at the 14,200-foot camp to report that a solo climber had been on the upper mountain for more than 24 hours and had not yet returned to his tent at high camp. NPS rangers notified Talkeetna personnel of the potential need for a search and rescue operation, which, due to weather and time of day, could not commence until the morning. The climber, Juergon Kanzia (41), from Austria, was last seen ascending from high camp to Denali Pass. There were no other climbing parties on the upper mountain at this time.

The NPS launched a full-scale search via ground and air that was in its second full day of operation when rangers at the 14,200-foot camp spotted what appeared to be a body below a long couloir below the summit plateau known as the Orient Express. The NPS contract helicopter with a ranger onboard flew to the site and confirmed that it did appear to be a body and the climbers clothing matched the description of the missing climber. Rangers and volunteers climbed to the site and recovered the body and assorted equipment and confirmed the identity of the missing climber. Events leading up to Kanzia's fall and death are not known. He had left his backpack and skis at a point close to the entrance to the Orient Express couloir and was apparently trying to descend on foot.

Analysis

The most significant contributing factor to this accident is likely the decision by Kanzia to ascend into severe weather and in the face of an unfavorable forecast. Other teams at high camp reported losing sight of the climber as he ascended towards Denali Pass due to the formation of a lenticular cloud over the upper mountain. Earlier conversations indicated that, although he was a very experienced climber and guide in other parts of the world, he seemed to be unfamiliar with big mountain weather and conditions factors. (Source: Coley Gentzel, Lead Mountaineering Ranger)

HAPE/HACE, FAILURE TO DESCEND
Alaska, Mount McKinley, Browne Tower

On the morning of June 29, Russian and American climbers Alexander Kharkovskiy (52) and Sergie Loz (58) began ascending from Browne Tower to an intended high camp on the upper Harper Glacier. An NPS patrol led by ranger Chris Erickson observed them to be moving extremely slowly, taking nearly six hours to move less than one half of a mile. The next day, the NPS patrol contacted the team while climbing past them on a carry. One of the climbers reported that his partner "wasn't feeling too well" and so was advised by the patrol to descend to a camp where his partner could better acclimatize. The team then slowly descended to Browne Tower, and at 2000, the partner returned to the NPS camp to request help for his sick teammate. The initial patient assessment, led by NPS Volunteer-In-Park Tom Gall (EMT-P), revealed that the patient had an SP02 of 46, resting HR of 120, and respirations 28/min, shallow and labored. Kharkovskiy and Loz were advised at this time to attempt to descend under their own power in the morning, as the patient could still walk and stand on his own.

The following morning, his oxygen saturation had worsened to 32 percent with all other vital signs remaining the same. NPS Physician-advisor Dr. Jennifer Dow was consulted via satellite phone and Albuterol, Diamox, and Dexamethasone were administered on the suspicion of High Altitude Pulmonary Edema (HAPE) and High Altitude Cerebral Edema (HACE). Through the course of the next 12 hours, 16 inches of snow fell on the Browne Tower camp and numerous signs of natural avalanches/slope instability were observed. Also during this time period, the patient's condition and vital signs did not improve, and at 1200 Mr. Gall reported that the patient was no longer able to stand on his own or walk under his own power. The patient's condition, the lack of available technical rigging supplies, the inability to mitigate the increasingly severe avalanche conditions, and an unfavorable weather forecast led the NPS patrol, in consultation with Dr. Dow and the Talkeetna ICS system led by John Loomis, to begin preparations for a helicopter evacuation.

The weather remained non-flyable for the rest of the day. On July 2, the clouds and snow lifted enough to allow the NPS helicopter to fly to Browne Tower, which lies at the top of Karsten's Ridge, an area that is consistently between 20 and 40 degrees in angle. A landing zone requiring approximately 24 labor-hours of digging and flattening was built and the helicopter was able to land there. At 1000, pilot Andy Hermansky, attended by Ranger John Loomis (EMT-P), departed with both climbers, one being uninjured yet considered to be unable to safely descend the crevasse-prone route on his own.

Analysis

Due to the length of approach and tougher glacial conditions, most parties move slowly on the Muldrow Glacier and are thus less likely to contract Acute Mountain Sickness, HAPE, or HACE. This expedition's pace was not considered overly fast. Regardless, the sick climber's health was clearly negatively affected by the altitude at Browne Tower. The team's one true error was that, despite the sick climber not feeling very well, they attempted to move up. Had they recognized the signs and symptoms of HAPE/HACE in the sick climber and decided to descend that day, they most likely would not have required NPS assistance. Given the remoteness of the Muldrow Glacier route and the fact that it is not patrolled as consistently as the West Buttress, the two climbers should are fortunate that help was so close and available at that time. (Source: Chris Erickson, Mountaineering Ranger)

(Editor's Note: In another case of illness, pneumonia, a climber whose life was not immediately threatened wanted a helicopter evacuation. The best means of treatment by medical personnel was to take antibiotics and descend on his own power—with his guides. The park clearly states its position with each expedition during the orientation. Here is an excerpt:

Denali National Park and Preserve recognizes that a certain number of park visitors each year will become ill, injured, or incapacitated in some way. It is the policy of Denali National Park and Preserve to assist those in need, when, in the opinion of the park personnel apprised of the situation, it is necessary, appropriate, within the reasonable skill and technical capability of park personnel, and provides searchers and rescuers with a reasonable margin of safety…

Denali National Park and Preserve encourages self-reliance, preventive education, and user preparation. We believe the prudent use of these elements to be the best possible means to safely enjoy the park.

The rangers on site during this episode said, "The NPS mountaineering rangers are on the mountain to protect the resource and to assist climbers in their time of need. This fact should not encourage climbers to rely on this safety net but instead to call for assistance when their team's rescue resources have been overwhelmed or depleted. This group had ample resources at their disposal to have dealt with this issue in a much more efficient and professional manner.")

FALL ON ROCK, UNFINISHED TIE-IN KNOT
Arkansas, Horseshoe Canyon Ranch

On October 8, a female climber on top-rope fell from near the top of what is believed to be Earl's Revenge (5.8). Unconscious but still breathing, she suffered a fractured forearm and possible spinal cord injury since she could not move her feet on command. She was carried on a backboard to a waiting helicopter and flown to the nearest trauma hospital.

According to witnesses, the cause of the accident was an unfinished tie-in knot. The climber tied her own knot, but unfortunately did not finish it. When she reached the anchors and sat in her harness, the knot came untied and she fell.

Analysis

Climbers in the area noted that the rope was detached from her harness, which was described as "new and intact". The rope end was found at the anchors with a figure-of-eight knot and working end of the rope trailing from the knot. Her partner did not check her knot.

As she was not wearing a helmet, she is beyond lucky that she sustained no head trauma.

Make sure both the climber and the belayer check knots, anchors, harness, etc. both visually and physically before starting any rock climb! (Source: Aram Attarian, edited from a post on rockclimbing.com.)

FALL ON ROCK – LOST CONTROL OF RAPPEL
Arizona, Oak Creek Canyon

On August 16, a man (36) was critically injured when he lost control of his rappel and fell more than 100 feet.

He was canyoneering, according to one report, and it took one set of rescuers seven hours to reach him, including seven rappels and three swim crossings at night. The entire rescue took 30 people and more than 2,200 feet of rope. They ended up raising him 450 feet to a ledge from which he could be short-hauled. (Source: Edited from an article and posting sent to us.)
(Editor's Note: No other incidents were reported from Arizona in 2011.)

FALL ON ROCK, RAPPEL ERROR – FAILED TO CLIP INTO ANCHOR
California, Joshua Tree National Park, Saddle Rock

On April 18, Dave Pinegar had lowered his partner from the route Walk on the Wild Side to the next anchor with his belay device. The partner clipped in to the anchor and yelled, "Off rappel." The next thing the partner knew was that Dave was flying by him. Dave was found at the bottom with the rope attached to his harness with a figure-eight on a bight tied at the mid-point of the rope.

Analysis

Dave Pinegar was an experienced climber from Germany. There are a couple of points here that should be clear. First, he obviously wasn't clipped into the anchor, and second, Walk On The Wild Side is usually a double-rope rappel with either 50 or 60-meter ropes.

A single 70-meter is pretty short for this task. Locals seem to concur that the 70-meter, single-rope rap is pushing it.

One news article said he was on a motorcycle trip, so maybe he just didn't bring his own gear. (Source: From a post on rockclimbing.com by Majid Sabetzadeh and an article in High Desert Star)
(Editor's Note: There were three other reports from J Tree. One was a fall on rock—no details, and the other two were rappel errors: one climber went off the end of the rope and the other climber fell because the ropes were uneven.)

STRANDED – ROPE STUCK, POOR COMMUNICATION – WIND, INEXPERIENCE
California, Yosemite Valley, Sunnyside Bench

After an hour of getting nowhere, Peter called the NPS for help. The ranger taking the call asked if Peter could rappel or Prusik down and free the rope. Peter replied that he didn't want to rappel and didn't know how to Prusik. Ranger Scott obviously didn't want to force the issue, so two rescuers responded. By the time they reached Nora, the stuck rope had been freed by another passing climber. Nora now had a safe upper belay but the rescuers found her clinging to the rock and afraid to move. Todd continued up to Peter, built his own anchor, and belayed both Nora and Colleen up the pitch. Everyone finished the climb and scrambled down the Sunnyside Bench descent path to the Valley.

Analysis

Nora was a beginner, so it was wise of her to be scared and careful. Peter claimed that he had several years of climbing experience at a high grade, including multi-pitch routes. The rescuers noted that he had an adequate anchor for himself and plenty of gear to descend, so not knowing what to do or how to do it was the likely culprit.

Peter and Nora were very appreciative of the rescuers' help, but one comment from Peter stuck in Ranger Scott's mind: "It's great to climb in the Valley. No matter how much trouble you get into you can just dial 911 for YOSAR." As long as Peter lacks basic self-rescue skills, we're likely to hear from him again. (Source: John Dill, NPS Ranger)

OFF ROUTE, FALL ON ROCK – PROTECTION PULLED WHEN WEIGHTED, INADEQUATE PROTECTION, COMPLACENCY
California, Yosemite Valley, Half Dome

On May 31, Maeve Devlin (19) and I, John-Mark Toth (22), hiked up to the classic Snake Dike route. From the base of the climb I led up the polished, low angle fourth class section to the 5.7 traverse that goes left under the roof. Here I placed my first piece, a .75 Camalot. "Bomber!" I thought. When I looked at the traverse, I saw hand and foot holds, so I started left, but after a few moves, it began to feel harder than 5.7— maybe 5.10a. I'd only climbed a few other pitches in Yosemite thus far and I thought, "Maybe this is a typical rating and it just feels harder." I was doing fine so I kept going. About 15 feet from the Camalot and 90 feet off the ground, with just one more move to the end of the tricky part, my left foot slipped. If you know anything about friction climbing you know this spells disaster.

I yelled, "Falling!" and turned around so I would slide on my butt. I looked at my protection, waiting for it to catch me. Much to my surprise, my placement wasn't so "bomber". The Camalot ripped off a two-foot by one-foot chunk of rock, leaving me with no protection at all. I managed to stay on my butt and slide feet first down the pitch, but I wasn't able to miss one little feature that caught my left foot and gave me my only serious injury—an ankle fracture. Not bad for falling 90 feet. I hit the ground. Luckily, my chunk of Half Dome hit a few feet to my left, also avoiding Maeve and a couple of other climbing parties.

I immediately knew I was hurt and everyone at the base started helping me. The rangers decided to fly me out because carrying me in a litter back to the trail was almost as difficult and risky as me exiting on my own. They advised me to keep my climbing shoe on the injured foot, which worried me, because if they later decided to cut it off, I would be very sad. While waiting for the helicopter I kept my foot elevated and packed in snow to help with the swelling. I surprised myself by staying in high spirits and making jokes to manage the pain.

The helicopter came back, I was hooked in, and we took off for the Valley. When we landed I made my shoe-cutting policy clear to the ambulance crew. Luckily they were also climbers and managed to save my TC Pros. At the hospital I learned that my fibula was broken in two places near the ankle.

Analysis

First, I should have doubled up my protection. I'd fallen on lots of trad gear with no failures before this one, but you can't fully judge the rock with only a whimpy tap or tug test. My piece looked so good that I didn't even consider a backup, though other placements were available. The easy climbing up to the roof and the fact that I can lead up to low 5.11 trad may have added to my complacency.

Second, I tried the "5.7" traverse 15-20 feet too high. My friends had climbed it and simply told me, "Go to the roof and go left," and I didn't notice on the topo that after placing protection under the roof, you drop down for the traverse. I looked over, saw holds, and nothing stood out as being an easier way. That's just the nature of climbing, and it's partly why I fell, but inadequate protection is why I broke my leg and hit the ground. (Sources: John-Mark Toth and John Dill, NPS Ranger)

FALL ON ROCK, PROTECTION CAME OFF
California, Yosemite Valley, El Capitan Muir Wall

Although I had climbed several walls in Zion, I had never climbed El Capitan; in fact, I had never even been to the Valley. Yosemite, and El Capitan in particular, had been built up in my mind, the ultimate destination and the ultimate goal.

Finally, on June 3, I arrived in Yosemite Valley with five weeks to climb. I carefully packed eight days worth of supplies, gear, ropes, and hardware into my haul bags, and within an hour of entering the Valley, I was humping loads to the base of The Captain.

After a day and a half climbing to the top of pitch eight, a gathering storm threatened several days of rain. I storm-proofed my gear and swung over to the fixed Heart Ledge rappels to head down to the valley floor. Three days of rest gave me time to decide if I was going to commit to the route. On June 8 I decided to head back up on the wall with two additional days of supplies.

After a couple more days of progress, I decided to take a rest day on a small sloping ledge below Pitch 24: the first crux. Now I was on to the upper pitches of the Muir and was starting to feel truly alone. There was a decent stance on a slab I used to set up and eat. I had enough supplies and the weather looked great for several more days. The past several days had been great, falling into the rhythm of solo climbing, sleeping well, and finding a peace I had been missing for quite a while.

On June 12 I went through the morning routine and got ready to lead Pitch 24, a classic thin nutting dihedral. I began the pitch with a #00 Black Diamond C3 and then placed two small DMM nuts. I then made a cam hook placement up to a yellow HB brass nut. Bouncing the nut resulted in some shift but I had confidence in the nuts body weight ability. Then I placed a green HB brass, more shifting, but it seemed fairly solid. I was getting close to a fixed Alien and I decided to place a cam hook to gain the fixed piece. As I tested the hook, several things went wrong in quick succession. The hook popped and I shifted onto the green HB with my fifi hook, shock loading the nut and pulling it out of the crack. As I fell, the next HB nut popped as well. My left foot hit the slab after I had fallen about 20 feet and I continued to fall about a body length as I crumpled onto the slab.

My left ankle hurt but nothing else. My head and spine seamed all right and I was able to move my neck with no pain. I stood up on the slab with my right foot and gingerly weighted my left foot. Instant blinding pain shot up my leg. I had fallen near the belay so I went to it and took off the gear rack. I dug out my day supplies bag and reached for the Ibuprofen and my cell phone. It was now 8:45 a.m.

I tried to call my oldest friend, climbing partner, and emergency contact, Jesse but the phone wouldn't dial out. I tried five, ten, a dozen times. I screamed at it, I pleaded with it, I begged it, and finally it dialed out. I had to hold the phone in a specific position for it to work.

I said that I was in trouble and told him that I thought I'd broken my ankle.

How quickly I had given up on the self-reliance of a solo ascent once a real problem reared its head. I could try and rappel the Muir. With the last few pitches being overhanging, and then several traversing pitches to regain Grey Ledges, I would have had to down-aid quite a bit. I also wondered if I could rappel over to The Nose. Making the rappels happen with the use of only one leg would be difficult and painful. The last option was to call YOSAR for a rescue. At the time, I did not want to consider this option. I was in the mentality of being a self-reliant climber. Jesse suggested we at least call YOSAR and make them aware of the situation. To save my phone we decided that Jesse would call them.

After fifteen minutes I got a call from Jack at YOSAR. After a quick assessment with an EMT, we started discussing the situation. Down-aiding was definitely going to be necessary to bail.

I set up my portaledge and took a closer look at my foot and ankle by removing my shoes and socks and placing my feet next to each other. It was obvious that my left ankle had a significant deformity. However, I could move my toes and circulation looked good. I began to think more seriously about a YOSAR rescue. I was still feeling like I should attempt to self-rescue. But doubts started to seriously enter my mind for the first time.

I called Jack back and he told me if I felt confident that I could self-rescue, I should. If not, YOSAR would begin mounting a rescue from the summit of El Cap. He also pointed out to me that if I got in trouble lower down on the wall, a rescue would only become more complicated for them. "I'll wait here for a rescue." I had three days of food and water left, which was good, because a more effective rescue effort could be mounted the next day. It was 11:30 a.m.

As soon as I got off the phone my mind started swirling. I was going to have to wait at least another 24 hours for rescue. I looked at the pitch above me. I felt failure and embarrassment. I knew that if I stopped moving, I would have to confront the reality of everything that had happened that morning. I cursed myself, I cursed El Cap, and I cursed Yvon Chouinard, TM Herbert, and Royal Robbins. I cursed climbing, cam hooks, and small nuts. I cursed myself again. I ate and drank. I got out my bivy gear and set up for the long wait. I wrapped my power-stretch around my foot and ankle for compression and splinted it using my wall hammer and athletic tape. I did everything I could think of.

I woke to a woman's voice saying "Matt....911." I realized with a jolt that she was talking to me from the valley with a loudspeaker. "Matt Seymour, if you can hear me raise one hand to acknowledge." The hand goes up. "If your phone still works dial 9-1-1." Soon I was on the phone with Jack again. The rescue was mobilizing.

At some point, I was looking out at the valley and casually looked up to see someone about 50 feet above me being lowered to my position. I got up and broke down my ledge. Jesse got to my ledge. He took my hand and shook it.

Analysis

A few things came out of the initial analyses that are worth noting. First, a cell phone turned out to be the most important piece of gear I had. Without it I would have been down to S.O.S. with a headlamp until someone saw me, but YOSAR would have had difficulty determining exactly what my problem was.

Another point on this is that I have a SPOT, but it was safely in my car. When the time came, to make the cell call, I had fairly poor service. The SPOT would have provided the backup.

Second, my level of medical training was not up to snuff. My front country First Responder certification was four years expired. If I had current training, I probably would not have missed the minor trauma to my head. After the rescue I was told they probably would have extracted me sooner had they known about the head injury. I ended with a fractured calcaneus and talus (which was also dislocated) and severely sprained ankle.

We want to see ourselves—and others—in our best moments. However, it is our failures that often truly shape us. Warren Harding climbed The Nose in part because he missed out on the first accent of Half Dome. I failed to climb El Capitan this time. But I have learned more about my goals and what motivates me than I have in a long time. (Source: Edited from a report written by Jason Seymour – 26)

STRANDED, FATIGUE, INADEQUATE WATER, INEXPERIENCE
California, Yosemite Valley, Royal Arches

On July 3, Cindy Lu (32) and I, Leo Wu (35), climbed Royal Arches. Despite it being our first really long climb, it had gone well. After starting at 5:30 a.m. we reached the first rappel at 4:30 p.m. Sunset was at 8:30 p.m., and we expected to be down in an hour or two, so we had plenty of daylight. We were happy and confident and looking forward to dinner, but by this time we were also exhausted and dehydrated. We had spent a long and very hot day in the sun with two liters of water each (plus keeping a third liter each in reserve for the descent), and we were climbing on three hours of sleep for each of the last three days, due mostly to travel from the East Coast.

We had no problems until we got to our seventh rappel, where there is only a tree with a bunch of slings and rap rings. Since all of the previous stations had been two or three-bolt anchors, I was expecting the same thing every time, so when I saw the tree anchor but no bolts, I thought I was off route. We were using double 60-m ropes so we had skipped a few anchors on the descent and no longer knew which rappel we were on. I figured we were OK because one station must lead to another, and since all the previous rappels had been straight down, I assumed this one would be too. (As we learned much later, we were at station No. 9 [SuperTopo] and should have rappelled down a ramp to the right, as shown on the topo.)

If I read the topo at all while I was at the tree I didn't figure it out. All I had in my mind was that I was off route but had a rappel station and two 60-m ropes, so I should be okay. I was so sure of myself that I never considered exploring the ramp. I told Cindy it might take a while to find the next station, and then I started rappelling. I didn't see anything for quite a distance, but that had been the case with earlier rappels, so I wasn't concerned. Finally, I saw two bolts with several slings directly below me, with an easy rappel from there to the huge ledge that is one rappel from the ground. So that had to be the right anchor, but when I got there, the ropes were two feet short, even with rope stretch. I had tied them together with two flat overhand bends with free ends maybe half a meter long, which I thought explained the shortage.

I considered ascending the rope back to the tree and exploring elsewhere. I had the basic knowledge to do that though I wasn't very skilled. But I was so sure this was the right anchor and I was so tired that I just wanted to get to the Valley. I extended the ropes with slings and tied the ends of the slings to my harness in case I fell. By shifting my weight temporarily to a friction hitch tied around the ropes, I managed to disconnect my rappel device and drop down hand over hand to the bolts. However, once my weight transferred from the ropes to the anchor, the ropes retracted up. I thought, "Wow, I screwed up. My plan is not going to work."

I didn't have a plan for the next step and I decided it was safer for Cindy to stay up by the tree until I figured out what to do. Perhaps an hour after I had left her, I called to her to stay where she was but we couldn't understand each other because of the wind. She thought I was yelling, "Cindy...rappel," so she started down after my tension was off the ropes. When she was halfway down she finally realized it was, "Cindy, do not rappel!"

When we could communicate— barely— I told her to stop and that I'd screwed up and didn't know what to do. We talked for a long time about our options and none of our options seemed right. I didn't want to make another mistake. It was almost dark as well, so we decided that Cindy would join me and we'd look for a way to retrieve the ropes. She came down and got onto the anchor. There were no footholds and we were crammed together hanging from the bolts only two pitches from the Valley floor. We tried to think of ways to get the ropes but I figured that it would either be risky in the dark or not possible, so I decided the only way out was to call for help.

We started flashing our headlamps. Someone near the hotel spotted us and soon the rangers were below us with a loudspeaker. They asked us if we needed help, and of course we said, "Yes" and told them we were uninjured. They asked if we were safe on our anchor (we were) and if we could stay the night.

We were very uncomfortable all night and shifted our positions every ten minutes to move the pressure points from our harnesses and maintain circulation in our feet. We got a little chilly despite our jackets and we were very thirsty. Even though we had one bottle of water left, we didn't dare to drink much, not knowing when the rescue would come. The worst for me were feelings of disappointment that I had made a bad decision and guilt from putting Cindy into this situation.

About 6:00 a.m. the next morning, two SAR guys free-climbed above us, rigged their ropes to a tree a little farther down the ramp, and rappelled to us. When we got down, Cindy and I had a big breakfast at the hotel and then slept until noon. By the next day my mood had improved. We climbed Nutcracker and enjoyed it as much as Royal Arches.

Analysis

As you can tell from the Leo's narrative, he and Cindy came away with lots of valuable take-home points. Here they are, along with some NPS comments:

• If you're relying on a topo then consult it thoroughly – but don't trust it blindly. As they learned much later, "We were at station No. 9 and should have rappelled down a ramp to the right."

• If your ropes come up short, either the anchor below or the one you're hanging from may be off route.

• Be aware of your mental state and that of your partner: tired, hungry, thirsty, frustrated, and/or focusing on home.

• Competence at ascending your rope is a core survival skill. To their credit, Leo and Cindy had at least introduced themselves to ascending with friction hitches, but they were inefficient at it and dead tired. Even after committing to his jury-rigged sling extensions—the ends of which he had wisely clipped to himself—he could have reversed his course with various rigging tricks.

• When they got home, Leo and Cindy bought family band radios. These may be the most reliable communication devices for climbs since they are independent of a network but cell phones may be better for seeking help where there's a chance you'll have service. If weight isn't an issue take both.

• A follower needs competency with every skill while protecting on the lead, including route finding, building anchors, rigging rappels, and ascending the rope.

• Leo felt he should have waited until he had more experience before trying Royal Arches. (Sources: Leo Wu and Cindy Lu; and John Dill, NPS Ranger.)

(John Dill: A similar incident occurred at the same anchor in November 2007, but while trying to reach the bolts the rappeller fell off her ropes and was seriously injured. See *ANAM 2008*.)

FALL ON ROCK, INADEQUATE PROTECTION, COMPLACENCY
California, Yosemite Valley, The Rostrum

On August 12th, my long time climbing partner (27) and I, Bud Miller (27), set off to climb the 1000-foot North Face of The Rostrum (8 pitches, IV 5.11c). The route was new to both of us and sure to push our limits, but it's considered relatively safe due to its protectable cracks and steep, clean falls. Although we weren't confident of on-sighting the route, at the worst we might take a few short falls.

To get to the route, you hike/rappel a steep gulley to the base, then after climbing to the top, it is a short hike up to the road. There seemed to be no reason to bring our approach shoes so we grabbed our gear and descended bare-foot.

Tommy took a short fall leading the 5.11 crux of Pitch 2, and I needed plenty of expletives to follow it. However, as self-proclaimed 5.10

climbers, this was no surprise, and we had forecasted a long day. At the belay we decided I would lead the next few pitches. Tommy passed me the rack and I took off.

Pitch 3 is long but not hard in relation to the rest of the climb. An initial 5.10 bulge is followed by a long 5.9 hand crack that starts thin and slowly widens. This grade and type of climbing had become comfortable for me after four months of climbing in Yosemite and to my stubborn mind it did not warrant throwing in much protection. So after the bulge I placed a green (.75) Camalot and climbed as fast as I could, never entertaining the idea of falling. As I got higher, I knew that I should add a piece but the pitch was so good that I just kept thinking, "Another move or two." Then, suddenly, my hand slipped out and I was falling backwards with plenty of time to realize that the Camalot was at least 25 feet below me. The piece held, but my fall, including rope stretch, was about 60 feet.

When I stopped I was hanging next to the belay. Tommy looked at me in horror; I looked back at him, upside down, and said, "I'm ok. My right foot is broken but I'm okay."

We stayed there half an hour, weighing options while I got my adrenaline under control. It was clear that my foot was 100% non-weight bearing, and whenever I bumped it the pain was excruciating. Prusiking the pitch after Tommy, negotiating the traverse, and scrambling one-footed up the gulley was to be avoided if we had another choice.

If we rapped the route, we faced crossing the Merced River to reach Highway 140 on the other shore. Although painful, the rappels went fairly smoothly. Scrambling down the forested scree slope from the climb to the river, perhaps 20 minutes on two good feet, took four hours. We made it with me sliding on my ass, Tommy holding me up on his shoulders, and fashioning a crutch with a stick, a shirt, and climbing tape.

The river was a mix of white water and deep, fast current and while Tommy could swim it, there was no way I could safely cross on my own. It was also out of the question to work our way up or down stream through huge boulders to a gentler crossing, so Tommy crossed with the climbing rope and some gear. He set up an anchor well upstream from where I was, fixed the rope, and then swam back with the loose end. We tightened the line with a Munter/Mule Hitch to give me a safe way to cross. I clipped a sling from my harness to the rope, hopped in the river, and pulled myself to the far shore. When we reached the road, we looked like characters out of Mad Max, but the first people we saw were kind enough to stop.

I had badly broken four metatarsals. After six months with a cast and physical therapy, I was back to climbing, hopefully a bit wiser.

Analysis

The reason I fell was the same reason I had under-protected, complacency due to over-confidence. I had climbed many cracks of this difficulty without ever falling, so I had begun to think I never would. Climbers usually place less gear on easier terrain but I discovered the hard way a reason for caution. (Source: Bud Miller and John Dill, NPS Ranger)

(NPS comment: Here are two other reasons for protecting more often: First, ratings are subjective. You never know, especially in Yosemite, when the rater's "5.9" pitch will surprise you. Second, placements fail, sometimes from user error and sometimes from an unnoticed fracture in the rock. The latter is true of handholds as well.)

FALL ON ROCK, OFF ROUTE, PARTY SEPARATED - CLIMBING ALONE, INADEQUATE CLOTHING, EXCEEDING ABILITIES
California, Kings Canyon National Park, Thunderbolt Peak

On August 21, Robert Levin (62), Steven Most (60's), and Mathew Most (20s) hiked from South Lake to camp in Dusy Basin in Kings Canyon National Park planning to climb Thunderbolt Peak (14,003-feet) in the Palisades via the Southwest Chute #2 route. After acclimating for two nights the group began their climb on the morning of August 23. They intended to climb a class 3 or 4 route without technical equipment. The group appears to have erroneously taken the Northwest Chute (class 4) on Starlight Peak rather than their planned route. About 1230 on August 23, Steven and Matt Most turned back because they felt the route was too exposed and more difficult than they were capable of. They attempted to convince Levin to join them, to no avail. Levin was determined to reach the summit and continued on without them. Two hours after the group separated, the Mosts heard Levin yelling, "Help!" from up on the peak.

Knowing neither the nature of Levin's predicament nor feeling technically capable of ascending the peak to assist, Mathew Most hiked to the trailhead to seek assistance while Steven Most remained near the base of the mountain at 11,000 feet.

A ranger hiked in on the morning of the 24th. The ranger heard occasional yells of "help" coming from below Thunderbolt Peak. Levin had spent the night alone, injured, with no equipment on a wall below the summit. He was wearing shorts, shirt, hat, and mountaineering boots. He had with him a fanny pack with one water bottle, energy bars and chocolate.

Levin was located after two hours of aerial searching in the vicinity of the West Rib route. He was perched on a two-foot sloping ledge, having fallen vertically over 100 feet.

Rangers Johnson and Corrao climbed fifth class terrain and reached Levin by 1800, thirty hours after the accident. He was dehydrated and hypothermic. Rangers stabilized him and due to approaching darkness prepared to lower him 100 feet into a sandy chute to bivy until a technical lower could be completed the following day. When a window of calm wind arrived, Levin was flown solo in a Bauman Screamer Suit to Ranger Erika Jostad at Barrett Lakes, packaged inside the helicopter, and flown to a hospital in Bishop, CA as dark descended.

He had suffered a concussion, open tibia-fibula fracture, and humerus fracture when he landed on his left side. Levin's humorous injury was surgically repaired. His left foot and lower leg were ultimately amputated due to the severity of the injuries and time elapsed between onset and treatment.

Analysis

Two of the three climbers recognized early on they had exceeded their abilities and equipment and were possibly off their intended route. Levin had lessened his safety net when he continued the summit attempt solo. The climber was unequipped for the terrain and was ultimately well off route on the descent. (Source: Ranger Erika Jostad, Kings Canyon National Park)

(Editor's Note: Each year we include one or two incidents in which hiking turns into a climbing situation. See Oregon, North Sister for another example.)

FALL ON ROCK – RAPPEL/LOWERING ERROR, POOR COMMUNICATION, HASTE

California, Tuolumne Meadows, Low Profile Dome

On September 12, Jody (27) and Karen (24) spent the day climbing in Tuolumne Meadows with friends Dan and Sanjay. In the afternoon they all hiked up to Low Profile Dome, a few minutes from the road. Jody and Karen climbed the Golfer's Route (5.7) while Dan led Family Affair (5.9) just to their left, and then Sanjay and Karen each followed Family Affair on a top-rope. (The two climbs share the same bolted anchor at the top of the routes about 180 feet above the ground and the top rope consisted of two climbing ropes tied together.) Finally, Jody top-roped Family Affair while Karen belayed from the ground. There were thunderstorms in the area and it was beginning to sprinkle; people were packing their gear and Jody recalls being in a hurry to finish the pitch and get down.

When she reached the top, Jody clipped to the anchor with a sling and called, "Off Belay." Then she untied, fed the rope through the anchor, retied it to her harness, and cleaned the party's gear from the anchor. Karen had been lowered from the climb previously, so Jody assumed she would also be lowered. She remembers calling, "I'm ready," and hearing Karen reply, "Okay."

At the base, Karen, Sanjay, and Dan heard Jody yell, "Off Belay." Karen replied "Belay Off" and removed the climbing rope from her belay device. She assumed that Jody would rappel since they had done that earlier in the day. No one on the ground remembers hearing Jody call, "I'm ready," or Karen responding "Okay." According to Karen and Sanjay, a few minutes after Jody called, "Off Belay," she yelled, "You got me?" Immediately after that— before Karen could say anything or put her back on belay— Jody screamed and fell. Somehow she stopped about 70 feet below the anchor, striking the back of her head on the rock.

No one is certain why Jody didn't fall all the way to the ground, since she was not on belay, but it appears that the rope snagged somehow. Karen had immediately and instinctively grabbed the rope and found herself holding Jody's weight, so she may have partially slowed the fall. Sanjay ran over and helped her hold on while she got Jody back on belay.

Jody was unresponsive and hanging horizontally in her harness. Several minutes later she regained consciousness and got herself upright, and Karen began to lower her. Meanwhile, a nearby group of climbers had seen the accident. Keith, a member of the group with a background in mountain rescue, climbed up the first pitch of the Golfer's Route and clipped himself to Jody. He tried to stabilize her head and neck as they were each lowered on separate ropes to the ground.

By the time the NPS arrived it was raining heavily. Jody knew her name and where she was but she responded slowly to questions. She complained of pain in her head, neck, and back, and also numbness in her extremities. The back of her helmet was cracked and covered in blood from a large scalp laceration. After immobilizing her, the NPS team carried her to the road and flew her to the park heli-base where she was transferred to an air ambulance. At the trauma center in Modesto she was diagnosed with a skull fracture and a relatively minor subdural hematoma. She has made a full recovery.

Analysis

Witnesses' memories vary regarding what was said and done but everyone involved agrees that a failure to confirm the descent plan was the direct cause of the accident. Karen and Jody were both moderately experienced at outdoor climbing and considered competent belayers. They met that morning for the first time through a mutual friend and climbed together all day. They did not have a descent plan in place before Jody began climbing Family Affair, and Jody says, "A major lesson for me...is the need to practice communications with your partner before you climb, especially if you haven't climbed together before." Despite being separated by a full pitch, Jody and Karen could hear each other, but Jody distinctly remembers rushing because of the rain and recalls, "I didn't communicate clearly that I was back on belay and ready to lower." Karen said, "When Jody fell, I thought I'd killed someone. It was an awful miscommunication. Her helmet saved her life." (Source: Jody and Karen; Alex Brun and John Dill, NPS Rangers)

(Editor's Note: See Colorado, May 17.)

FALLING ROCK – PULLED FLAKE OFF, FALL ON ROCK, OFF-ROUTE, HASTE
California, Yosemite Valley, Half Dome
Early in the morning of September 19, Markus Praxmarer (48) and Thomas Wanner (30) began a one-day ascent of the Regular Northwest

Face route on Half Dome (23 pitches, VI 5.9 C1). A New Zealand party preceded them and two other groups, Canadian and Swiss, followed. Praxmarer led the first block of pitches with Wanner planning to take over the lead at pitch 10.

As he started leading pitch 7, Praxmarer traversed right and began climbing through an area of large flakes. He was 30 feet up and right from the belay, with the rope clipped through three pieces of protection, when Wanner saw a "body-sized" flake come loose as Praxmarer was climbing over it and pulling on it. Wanner felt a quick tug on the rope but nothing more, and he was surprised when Praxmarer continued to fall past him, 700 feet to ground.

The parties below saw Praxmarer and several rocks fall past them. One of the Swiss called the NPS while a physician in their group rappelled and confirmed that Praxmarer had died instantly of massive trauma. The New Zealand party also witnessed the fall from their position just above Praxmarer on the same pitch. They descended to Wanner and rappelled with him to the ground.

Analysis

Apparently Praxmarer and the flake fell together and when the lead rope came tight, the flake was right above it. The flake's momentum severed the rope just in front of Praxmarer's harness. When Wanner looked at the topo after the accident, he saw that the usual pitch went up and left, so he realized that Praxmarer was probably off-route. They were close behind the New Zealanders, and when they went to the right the Austrians assumed they were on route and followed without checking the topo. The New Zealanders reported the climbing in that area to be harder than they had expected from the topo, and based on one of Wanner's photographs, Praxmarer may have been aiding, perhaps putting more force on the flake than he intended. It's also likely that more loose rock exists off the normal route than on it. Praxmarer and Wanner had climbed other Yosemite routes, including The Nose on El Capitan, and they guided professionally in Europe, so there's little doubt that Praxmarer understood the danger and unpredictability of loose rock. (Source: Ed Visnovske and John Dill, NPS Rangers)

PROTECTION PULLED WHEN WEIGHTED – FALL ON ROCK
California, Yosemite Valley, El Capitan

On September 26, Michael Schmoelzer (52) and Ritchie Edelsbacher (44), both experienced climbers from Austria, were in their third day of an ascent of The Nose (31 pitches, 5.9 C1). By 3:00 p.m. they had passed the Great Roof and Schmoelzer was leading Pitch 23 to Camp V.

Michael Schmoelzer: I was about 65 feet above Ritchie, aid climbing the main crack in the corner, when I had to switch to another crack on my left. That crack angled up and right until it joined the main crack several moves above me. My last piece in the main crack was a small cam. From there I reached out three or four feet to the left crack and placed a small stopper. I tested it, moved onto it, and clipped my rope to it with a long quickdraw. I stepped up in my aider and placed a second small stopper about three feet above the first. I attached an aider and tested the piece. It moved a little bit, but it seemed like it would hold body weight. I clipped my rope through it with a shorter quick draw and stepped up again, but when I did so, the rope tension pulled the nut out. As I fell, the angle of the rope from the cam pulled the lower nut out sideways. It had been solid for the move but not for the fall. The cam held, and Ritchie had no problem stopping me after I'd fallen about 15 feet. I was hanging maybe 40 to 50 feet above the belay.

I wasn't surprised that the upper nut had pulled out, although I hadn't expected the lower nut to fail as well. The fall was smooth and nothing to be concerned about. I didn't hit anything, and the stop was gentle. As I fell, however, I felt something—a rope, or sling, or cord—dragging over and pulling on my right hand. It was a little painful in my fingers, and as I found later, it had deeply cut two-thirds of the way around my ring finger. Whatever had grabbed me quickly slid off my fingers and the pain had stopped. As I was hanging on the rope afterward I had no pain anywhere and appeared to have no serious injuries.

Then I saw blood on my face and my pants and I didn't understand why. I looked down to see where it was coming from and found that my right thumb was missing. It was torn off between the two joints, with bone showing and blood shooting out of the end, like from an artery. I held my hand high, and the bleeding stopped within a minute, but I was amazed because I had not felt pain in my thumb. It must have happened very fast, for as I had fallen all I had noticed was the pain in my fingers.

I called to Ritchie, "Did you see my thumb?" He said, "Yes, it's lying here next to my feet." He had known before I did because he had seen it falling and recognized it immediately as a thumb. It had tumbled from near my high point and had landed within a foot or two of his feet. The funny thing is that when he saw the thumb he thought, "How shall I express this to Michael without frightening him too much?" So he said nothing until I called to him.

Ritchie lowered me to the ledge, and I clipped in. He put my thumb into a Ziploc bag and into his pocket. We pretty quickly decided to request a helicopter, although air access would be difficult because the cliff was very steep where we were. Our hope was to get my thumb and me to a surgeon soon enough to permit a successful reattachment. As I started to call the 112 international emergency number—good in the USA, as well—I found myself unable to remember it. I must have been a little bit in shock because I am a mountain rescuer and should know this number. Fortunately Ritchie, also a rescuer, recalled it.

I had to lean out of our corner to get cell access. The signal was weak but about one hour after the accident, I managed to reach a park dispatcher, who informed the rescue team. We asked if we should rappel or wait for the helicopter. We were advised to wait for an air rescue attempt. We decided that if this plan failed we would rappel, but we would not be able to complete the descent until morning because one of our headlamps had failed.

While we waited, we cut the sleeve off my jacket so I could put it on against the chill. I also took my thumb back from Ritchie, as I certainly didn't want to leave it behind if I got rescued. We thought about bandaging my hand but decided not to. The bleeding had stopped, I was comfortable with it uncovered, and I was concerned about putting pressure on the bone. We didn't know what to expect from the rescuers, so we organized our equipment and ropes to avoid problems from the helicopter's rotor wash.

NPS: When we got word of Michael's situation we made two plans. First, we would try to take him directly off the wall by helicopter. Second, if that turned out to be too difficult and risky, we would allow enough time before dark to fly rope rescuers to the summit. They would lower a medic to Michael and possibly continue lowering Michael and the medic to the ground.

After a recon flight, the air rescue team decided that conditions were satisfactory for the primary plan. The park helicopter hovered 30-40 feet to one side of their belay ledge and well above it, with two rescuers suspended on a short-haul line. The aircrew was able to throw a weighted tag line over to Ritchie. One rescuer, Dave, clipped Michael to the short-haul line, released him from the belay anchor, and signaled the helicopter. It flew Dave and Michael back to the meadow, where Michael and his thumb (now on ice) were transferred to a waiting air ambulance. Jeff stayed with Ritchie and they were raised to the summit by the rescue team the next morning.

Michael: (I)…was transported to the California Pacific Medical Center in San Francisco by midnight and was ready for surgery at 1:00 a.m. They reattached the thumb, and three days later the circulation was the same as in my undamaged fingers. Today, several months later, my thumb is completely healed, although I cannot bend the tip due to damage to the joint.

Analysis

In the hospital the day after the accident, I sketched the scene to try to figure out what happened. Just before I fell, my right hand may have been somewhere on the quick draw or on the hand sling attached to the top of the aider. My aiders—with fifi hooks attached—were tied to my harness with long, 3mm keeper cords, so they fell with me. My lead rope crossed in front of me from the cam on the right to the first nut on the left and what I felt on my hand was similar to the rough texture of my rope. Some or all of those pieces of equipment may have tangled with other gear and then somehow surrounded and squeezed my hand as I fell. The 3mm cords, being narrow, would most easily have cut into my hand, but I really don't know the answer.

I'm a climbing instructor for children six to 15 years old in my alpine climbing club, and I always say, "Hands off the rope when you fall!" This is so simple, and I thought I tried to get my hands off. I have a story to tell them now, and a thumb to show off.

My second piece of advice is for foreign climbers coming to the USA: Double-check that your accident insurance is the proper one, with lots of coverage. Very important. Look carefully at the clauses of the insurance contract.

Third, you may think this was a unique accident, but you should read John Robinson's story in *ANAM 2011*. It involves the same route, the same injury from an aid fall, and the same amazing recovery and reattachment of his thumb. (Source: Michael Schmoelzer and John Dill, NPS ranger)

(NPS Note: Take Michael's advice. The NPS does not charge for rescue costs, although there are typical charges for medical care in the field and at the park's clinic. However, a commercial air ambulance fee from the park to Modesto can exceed $25,000 and at least two climbers seriously injured recently in Yosemite have incurred hospital bills of over $500,000.)

FALL ON ROCK, INADEQUATE PROTECTION
California, Yosemite Valley, Washington Column

On September 27, Taylor Sincich (23) and I, Tommy Bairstow (24), set out to climb Mid-East Crisis on the east face of Washington Column. I had fixed four pitches by myself two days earlier, and we hoped to finish it off in a day. Working in the Valley had allowed me to crank out 11 big walls in the previous six months, but this would be the last for a while— the start of a relaxing sabbatical.

We jugged the fixed lines, and after I led pitches five through eight as a block, Taylor took the rest. We were using a 60-m lead line and a 60-m x 10-mm static tag line, the latter for lower-outs, shuttling gear, and retreat if necessary. The follower carried our daypack containing water, lights, and cell phones, so we had no haul bag. By 2 p.m. we were in the huge, multi-pitch system of overhangs above the Great Slab. After completing Pitch 10, Taylor pulled up the slack, anchored the lead line to the bolts, and called for me to come up.

Pitch 10 was drastically traversing and overhanging, so cleaning was tricky and exhausting. It took much longer than usual, and Half Dome was glowing gold by the time I neared the belay. This meant we had about one hour of light with 2.5 pitches to go, so I was moving fast, though not carelessly. The last placement to clean was a #4 cam about five feet below the anchor and two or three feet to its left. "Almost there," I thought. Just a routine move around the piece and then I could relax at the anchor. I could see Taylor watching me as I prepared to clean the cam.

At this point I was hanging completely free of the wall on the lead rope. Both feet were in aiders connected to the lower, left-hand jug (my usual rig) and the upper jug was on the rope just under the cam. Both jugs were connected to my harness with daisies. The ends of the lead rope were tied to our belay loops, and the tag line was tied between the haul loops on the backs of our harnesses. Per my standard practice, I was not tied in short, so almost the entire lead rope and tag line each hung in a long loop below me.

My plan was to weight the lower jug and then remove the upper one and reattach it above the cam. Then I would shift my weight to the upper jug, remove the cam, and finish climbing a few feet to the anchor. I've re-lived this moment a thousand times in my head: I reached for my top jug, grabbed the trigger, and immediately started falling—and kept falling.

At first I thought the #4 cam had blown but that would only have swung me out a bit. Or maybe the anchor had failed. I started screaming. I've been told I have a high-pitch to my voice when I fall. "I'm gonna die!! I'm gonna die!" must have sounded strangely boyish to Taylor.

I hit something almost immediately—a small slab about 50 feet beneath me that barely jutted out—and it shot me further outward. My feet absorbed most of the impact, and it felt like dynamite going off in my left boot. My new Sportiva high-tops were ejected from my feet. (They were later found at the base with the left shoe still tied.) The impact had no time to register, as I was immediately in free fall again. I had taken my fair share of short falls before, but to fall so far with no warning was utterly terrifying. Why was I falling? The Great Slab was getting closer. I felt a strange acceptance and thought, "I guess this is it."

And then I slowed to a stop, dangling in space just above the slab. The lead rope had held. I had fallen about 170 feet and all those thoughts had occurred in a few seconds. Thanks to the dramatic steepness of the route, the fall had been almost completely clean. That moment I stopped was like a rebirth, with screaming, tears, and a profound sense of joy and luck. I wasn't dead, but I was injured, and my first thought was of rescue. Furthermore, I could see at least two core shots (cuts completely through the sheath) in the lead rope just above me, and I wondered if the line would snap.

After making a panicked 911 call, I managed to gather myself into coherency. I talked to Search and Rescue, talked to several of my climber friends around the Valley, and even talked to myself a bit. Jack, the ranger at SAR, asked me several medical questions to confirm that my worst injury was the left ankle and that it still had circulation, feeling, and movement. It was too close to dark for helicopter support and it would take hours to hike a team to the summit and lower a rescuer to me. Furthermore, the team was dealing with a climbing accident at Higher Cathedral Spire that might be more serious than mine, so he asked if I could jug to the anchor and even follow Taylor to the top if I felt up to it. I was hanging in my harness, not a good place for the night, so I was willing to give it a try. We arranged to stay in touch and hung up.

I surveyed my injuries. My left ankle was the size of a softball, throbbing severely, definitely broken, and utterly useless. My right ankle was sprained but still had movement and flexibility; it would be painful but I could use it, though I had nothing on my feet but socks. My fingertips were burned and blistered from trying to grab the rope when

I started falling, but I was wearing gloves so my hands were spared. I was almost out of water and the light was fading. "Okay." I said out loud to myself, "This is going to be the hardest thing you've ever done."

I yelled, "Taylor!"

"You okay? What's up?"

"My ankle is broken, my fingertips are burned. I think I'm gonna jug up to you."

"Okay man, just be safe."

After an eternity I made it to the anchor and put Taylor on belay. I felt like I might pass out, and of course that worried Taylor, since he was leading, but I belayed with a Grigri. The bigger issue may have been relying on our core-shot and burnt-sheath lead rope, but the remaining pitches were short enough to keep the core shots out of the system.

Taylor finished the pitch and rappelled the tag line. Then he lowered me out so I could ascend the free-hanging tag line as he cleaned on the lead line. In the distance below I could see headlamps starting up North Dome Gully, which meant that our friends were scrambling up with food, water, and painkillers. Their shouts and light flashes brought a tremendous wave of relief. We just had to get to the top.

After the last technical lead, pitch 12, Taylor was too tired to rappel to me and clean, so we left everything there for him to retrieve someday. Jugging that pitch forced me to drag my broken ankle up a slab for 120 feet. Each time it banged against the rock was like breaking it all over again.

We were exhausted and dehydrated, but our friend Isaac had down-climbed the final 100 feet to bring us some water. He fixed the tag line to the top of the climb, and Taylor and I crawled slowly up, with plenty of cursing and screaming on my part. It was about 1:00 a.m. My friends were Wilderness First Responders, but it didn't take any medical training to realize that hiking out was impossible for me. They called SAR back, updated them on my condition, and made plans for a rescue.

In the morning I was short-hauled off the top of the Column by the SAR chopper and taken to the Yosemite clinic. I was released later that day with a broken and dislocated left talus bone and some bandaged fingers, but otherwise fine. After surgery and six months of sometimes painful healing, I'm pretty close to full strength, and hopefully I'll be a safer climber. I was extremely lucky.

Analysis

Tommy said, "I have never used a back-up system in my ascending. I'm mainly a self-taught wall climber, and this made sense to me. Foolish. From now on I will ALWAYS back up my ascending." He also indicated that none of his partners had ever stressed to him how crucial it was to back up his ascenders. After watching Tommy clean Pitch 9, Taylor did suggest that he clip a 'biner through the hole in the top of his ascenders and asked, "Do you do any backups?" But Taylor is a polite fellow and didn't push the issue or suggest tying in short to the rope.

We know that climbers don't always back themselves up while ascending, both in Yosemite Valley and elsewhere, but this has resulted in several accidents that were otherwise preventable. The discussion following Tommy's trip report on SuperTopo.com is one place to start. (Search trip reports for Crisis in Yosemite.)

We hope that both of them will be a bit more aggressive when providing advice to their climbing partners after this incident.

A couple of self-rescue suggestions. After a fall like Tommy's, consider providing a belay with the tag line, and even a counter-weight haul, to protect and assist your freaked-out partner as he ascends the potentially damaged lead line. In addition, Tommy was carrying both cell phones and both headlamps in the daypack. Now they each carry their own all the time. (Source: Tommy, Taylor, and John Dill, NPS Ranger)

VARIOUS FALLS ON SNOW – CAUSES INCLUDED OFF ROUTE, SEPARATED FROM GROUP, INADEQUATE FOOTWEAR (SNEAKERS), ICE AXES ON PACKS, FALLING ROCK, AND ONE HAPE FATALITY
California, Mount Shasta, Avalanche Gulch

The five climbing incidents on Mount Shasta were in the usual location: Avalanche Gulch.

The causes generally involved an inability to self-arrest or to continue on. The falling rock case resulted in a 300-foot fall and an open fracture. There was one HAPE fatality that occurred on the Clear Creek Route. Another curious fatality—not climbing-related—happened when an individual who was part of a religious/ceremonial group decided to hike on his own "to place a rock on top of the mountain." He was eventually found in the upper Old Ski bowl area. He was wearing sweatpants and a light shirt and wore no shoes.

The climbing ranger report indicated the following: Mount Shasta had a similar season to the 2009-10 winter with a strong La Nina pattern influencing weather patterns and brought an above normal precipitation to the region. Snow accumulation was 164% of the historical average for 2011. Similar to last season, our spring was disguised with winter weather, cooler temperatures, and above normal precipitation through June. This caused late winter climbing conditions to extend into the beginning of July, which meant firm, smooth snow, making for good climbing but very dangerous if a fall is taken and self-arrest is not immediately performed successfully. As a result, the conditions were ripe for several searches and rescues. Climbing conditions remained in good shape through September. (Source: Nicklaus Meyers, US Forest Service Lead Climbing Ranger & Avalanche Specialist)

DISLODGED ROCK – FALLING ROCK
Colorado, Shelf Road

I was belaying my partner on January 16. We were climbing a new route not in the guidebook when he kicked off a baseball-sized rock from approximately 60 feet up. It made a direct hit, striking the center of my skull! Luckily I was wearing a helmet. We recognized the potential for loose rock before getting on the climb.

Analysis

My partner and I were the only climbers wearing helmets all weekend. It's your choice not to wear one. Personally I'm happy to wear one, even for casual, one-pitch sport-cragging. Head injuries can be very serious and I'd like to avoid them. If you don't own one or don't wear the one you have, maybe you should consider it. (Source: Ryan Kane from a post on mountainproject.com)

AVALANCHE, NO BELAY ANCHOR
Colorado, Ten Mile Canyon, The Shroud

During the mid-morning of January 17, while two climbers were top roping The Shroud ice climb (WI3-4), an avalanche from above the climb flowed through the area. The climber on the ice at the time was generally protected just below the top of the ice flow and the avalanche ran over him. The belayer was not anchored and was swept from his belay stance. The belayer was unable to hold the break on the belay device and slid approximately 30 feet down the rope where a knot stopped him from being carried away by the avalanche and releasing the climber above. The snow flowed over the climber and pummeled the belayer for approximately ten seconds and then continued past the climbers.

Neither party was injured or buried, as the two climbers held each other's weight at the end of the rope through the secure top-rope anchor. The slide reached the bike/ski/snowshoe path at the base of the slope approximately 400 to 500 feet below. (Source: Colorado Avalanche Information Center: avalanche.state.co.us)

Analysis

A closed belay system and a secure top rope anchor may have made a difference in the outcome of this incident. Climbers are encouraged to check avalanche reports before attempting any climb in avalanche terrain. (Source: Aram Attarian)

FALL ON SNOW, UNABLE TO SELF-ARREST, FAILURE TO TURN BACK, EXCEEDING ABILITIES
Colorado, Rocky Mountain National Park, Mount Meeker

On Saturday, January 29, Eric, Ward, Ned, Arnold and I were planning on attempting Mount Meeker (13,911 feet) via the Iron Gates route that eventually diverges from the Chasm Lake trail and follows a generally Class-2 ridge to one of the summits. The weather was gorgeous—warmer and sunnier than we possibly could have hoped—and the high winds in the area had scoured most of the alpine area around Meeker and Longs Peak clean. The snowpack was hard and stable, so for the most part, we could not punch through and we did not have to posthole through the patches of snow that we did encounter.

We continued along the Chasm Lake trail as it winds around Mount Lady Washington and follows a path cut into a steep slope. The area is cliffed-out in sections directly off the path. These portions of the trail were covered in snowdrifts, making them trickier than in the summer by far. We took out our ice axes and some of us donned crampons. The trail eventually cleared out and we reached a snowfield above Peacock Pool that stretched to Chasm Lake. There were steps cut into it already from a previous party. The snowfield was steep (approximately 30-40 degrees) and covered the landscape in a large south to southeast-facing bowl that led to a boulder field below. We assessed other options to avoid crossing the snowfield. We discussed descending to the bottom of the cirque and climbing up the edge of Columbine Falls, or following a different path on the snowfield lower down. We decided to proceed onto the [icy] snowfield. Temperatures in the area were well above freezing the preceding day and well below freezing during the morning. Thus the early morning south-facing snow surface was icy.

Ned and Ward put on their crampons (Eric, Arnold and I already had them on), and Ward led us out onto the snowfield spaced ten feet apart, following the pre-kicked steps that were already there. Next in line were Ned and Arnold. I followed behind them with Eric behind me. After completing a mountaineering course this summer and gaining technical training with crampons and ice axes, I believed I would be able to arrest my fall if I were to slip.

At this point, the events of the day are very hazy for me. What I have managed to piece together is the result of the fast-paced experience I endured and the accounts of Eric, who was forced to watch the entire process in abject horror and helplessness.

Probably ten to twenty steps onto the snowfield, I fell on the hard snow. I found myself completely underprepared for arresting a fall. I gained speed very quickly and tried to flip over and weight my pick into the snow to stop myself. The pick scraped the snow, and then ripped out of my hands due to the force and speed of my fall. After traveling roughly 100 feet and picking up speed, I impacted a rock jutting out of the snow with the bottom of my left thigh. I caught air and continued another 20 feet into the boulder field below, where I finally stopped my fall.

The impact of the blow was reverberating throughout my entire body. Sharp, grueling pain began in my left hip and back and I began to go into shock and to hyperventilate. The hyperventilation caused my fingers and toes to tingle, something I had been told to look for as a sign of spinal cord damage. My left thigh had suffered a major abrasion (sic) through which I would eventually lose a pint of blood, but I did not notice at the time. At this point, Eric had run down the slope to me, and Ned, Arnold, and Ward were close behind. Eric took out his SPOT and asked me if he should press the button that would send for help.

Although the idea of needing to press the SPOT was unfathomable, I knew that I needed a backboard, and an evacuation. There was no way I could possibly walk down the mountain. It was roughly 8:00 a.m.

I was moved onto an insulated surface. Arnold and Ned began to head towards the trailhead with incredible speed and competency to call 911, asking anyone traveling up the trail if they had cell phone service. These travelers proved to be invaluable as they came across Eric, Ward, and I, and told us of our friends' progress towards the trailhead. Arnold and Ned had left their warm layers with me, and had moved as quickly as possible to get help, call my parents, and send for a backboard.

Around 10:00 a.m., Rocky Mountain National Park Search and Rescue [rangers] made contact, and the next stage of the ordeal began. It would take me fifteen hours to reach the trailhead.

For me, the entire rescue was a series of jostling bumps, caring assessments, checking of vital signs, and half-conscious experiences. I arrived at the trailhead at 11:30 p.m., accompanied by the exhausted rescue teams that had worked so hard to save my life. The rescue teams had been working to evacuate me for 15 hours. I was immediately taken to the Estes Park ER. X-Rays were taken and I was cleared for movement. I breathed a sigh of relief. My spine was okay but I was confused by the unexplained and intense pain in my lower back that completely eclipsed the laceration in my leg. I was given Vicodin and kept in the hospital for the remainder of the morning: the doctors were concerned about the possibility that the muscle damage to my leg could cause kidney damage. By the morning, my kidneys were on the right track, but we discovered that my lungs had collapsed slightly from being bound into the litter for so long. (NB: Probably atelectasis, not true lung collapse – J.D. Forrester)

An orthopedist revealed that I had fractured my sacrum, the extension of my spine that connects to my pelvis.

Analysis

The lessons that can be learned from this are complex and multi-faceted. As hikers and mountaineers, we often take risks and find ourselves in situations where we could have died. Had I failed to hit the rock, I would have hurtled into the boulder field full-force. Had I impacted the rock with my head, or anywhere near my internal organs, I could have died on or shortly after impact. Had the impact on my back been different, or the avalanche shovel failed to protect me, I could have been paralyzed or dead. For the first time, and hopefully the only time, I find that I not only could have died, but truly should have died in countless ways this past weekend. Also note: a SPOT device is not a true safety net. If I had suffered internal bleeding or a more serious injury, I would have died before I made it into town. The wilderness is not a button away from front-country medicine.

In the process of pushing ourselves, we often hear voices that tell us "this isn't such a great idea" or maybe caution us of potential consequences if we miss a step. The situation I found myself in this weekend was rare, but we face situations where we gauge risk versus reward almost every weekend we spend in the mountains. I am pleading with you to have the courage to turn back. I know the pressure of trying as a trip leader to fulfill group expectations of grandeur, and I know the feeling of being a participant and not wanting to hold back a group. Travel with people you know would accept your discomfort and acknowledge objective hazards and respect them. If someone says they are uncomfortable with a situation, listen. Realize that the people you travel with in the mountains may be the ones who save your life. (Source: Rebecca Stubbs -29 from a post on rockymountainrescue.org)

(Editor's note: The ability to self-arrest a fall on steep snow varies with individual experience and skill, equipment, and snow surface conditions. While perhaps not obvious, it is well established that after falling on steep, icy snow, it is nearly impossible to self-arrest. An additional hazard, that did not come into play in this case is that when attempting self-arrest with crampons on, it is easy to catch the front points, which always exacerbates the fall.)

FALLING ROCK, FAILURE TO TEST HOLD, SEATED BELAYER
Colorado, Shelf Road

Despite the rain and a recent shoulder dislocation, Joe (32) and Chris (35) decided to keep their plans to climb at Shelf Road to celebrate the end of a hard semester of grad school. Joe was interested is scoping out the area and they were glad that the injury would force Chris and their friend Holly to lead routes without Joe.

Record rains that week pushed Cañon City over the normal annual rainfall mark. After setting up camp on May 14, Chris put up several short routes and found a few loose bits of rock but no major shifts in the rock. Rain on May 15 kept the group, now joined by Holly, to sightseeing and feasting at camp.

May 16 was beautiful and sunny by 10:00 a.m. After packing up camp the group joined a dozen or so groups in the canyon for some easy 5.6-5.8 routes. Chris and Holly were enjoying the challenge of leading all the routes and Joe was able to TR a few. They had found a moderate dihedral with about six or seven bolts on the Piggy Bank wall likely to the right of Piñon Slalom. They were using Rock Climbing Colorado: Falcon Guide that does not give much detail to each area.

After Chris made it past the second bolt, Joe sat down to belay against a perfectly situated tree. About 3:30 p.m., Chris reached the anchor bolt, but she hadn't clipped in or called down, "Safe (sic)." Joe was looking left to talk with their mutual climbing partner. Chris opted to reach high as she prepared to clip into the anchor while she stood on a secure, but small ledge. Without testing the block, she pulled and with little effort it came loose and quickly gained speed. Chris shouted, "Rock!" to alert Joe, but because of his reclining position and little decision time, he could only role off to one side. The 20-pound rock fell unhindered for over 45 feet.

Joe tucked to avoid being struck in the head and rolled left. The crushing force of the stone was surreal as it compressed his body. Striking first his left shoulder blade, the rough limestone dug several lacerations and scrapes. The left quadriceps seemed to take the majority of the force—almost catching the block. He stopped laying face down ten feet from his original belay seat.

Joe was conscious and held onto the belay, expecting Chris to be pulled from her stance by his rolling. In terror, Chris watched an event that she thought would kill her beloved. She was stable on the ledge, but did not secure herself promptly. Joe tried to communicate to Holly to make sure the area was safe, call for help and for someone to take the belay. Joe was using his BD ATC Guide belay/rappel device rather than the Grigri in their pack. After the initial shock, Chris was able to secure herself into the anchor using a PAS.

Moments later other climbers responded to the commotion. The first couple on the scene was a newly certified EMT and his WFR-trained partner. Someone took over the belay while the EMT did a head-to-toe examination of Joe. It was deemed that Joe had not suffered any head or back injuries and was helped to a seated position. Severely shaken, Chris was lowered and cleaned the route.

The amazingly mild injuries sustained during this accident allowed Joe to hike out a quarter mile aided by several other climbers to a vehicle that had been driven into the area. At the hospital it was confirmed that there were no broken bones, head or spinal injuries. Bruised ribs, a contusion of the left quadriceps, a laceration on left shoulder blade and a small puncture wound on the left ankle were the only injuries sustained. The bruised ribs took eight weeks to heal.

Analysis

Test every hold, even in a well-traveled area. Climbing above a standard route will likely be unclean and loose. Do not sit during a belay if at all possible to give greater agility. An auto-locking belay device, if used correctly, can greatly increase the safety if the belayer were to be rendered unconscious. (Source: Edited from a report by J. Black)

FALL ON ROCK – POOR COMMUNCATION
Colorado, Clear Creek Canyon

On Tuesday May 17, American Alpine Club (AAC) Executive Director Phil Powers (50) took four of his employees—Keegan Young, Penn Burris, Sarah Wood, and Deanne Buck—climbing at High Wire Crag in Clear Creek Canyon, a popular and accessible sport climbing area near the AAC headquarters in Golden. The group had varying levels and numbers of years of climbing experience. The goal of the day was team building and preparation for a two-day climbing retreat they had planned for early June.

Upon arrival at the crag, Powers led Cracker Jack (5.8) with Wood belaying him from the ground. He attached two quickdraws to the anchor chains, ran the rope through quickdraws, and was lowered to the ground. Next, Wood climbed Cracker Jack on top rope with Powers belaying. Wood removed the intermediate quickdraws as she climbed the route. She left the quickdraws in place at the anchor and was lowered to the ground. Powers then climbed Bypass (5.10), the route to the immediate right of Cracker Jack on top rope. Wood again belayed Powers from the ground. Powers and Wood had not discussed whether Powers would rappel or be lowered. In addition, the area where the group was climbing is directly above the highway and river. Verbal communication once Powers was climbing was difficult and, once above an overhang, he was out of the belayer's view.

When Powers reached the anchor, he decided to thread the rope directly through the permanent chains to avoid having a less experienced climber clean the anchor later in the day. He shouted for slack. Wood heard his call and fed him some rope. Wood then thought she heard Powers call, "Off belay." Wood paid out rope but kept Powers on belay to make sure he was intending to rappel.

Once the rope was threaded through the anchor, Powers decided to place an intermediate anchor or directional (quickdraw) high on Cracker Jack to improve the rope placement for the next climber. The rock was low angle, so Powers was able to down-climb about 20 feet. He placed a quick draw on the second-to-last bolt on Cracker Jack. The action of the rope as Powers was down-climbing seemed to Wood as if he was pulling up rope to arrange a rappel. Wood again thought she heard, "Off belay," so she removed the rope from her belay device and called up to Powers that he was off. At the same moment, Powers clipped the rope into the directional quickdraw, called for tension, leaned back on the rope and fell 70 feet to the ground.

Powers' companions administered first aid immediately and runners were sent down to the road to and up to a high point for a cell signal. The Golden Fire Department responded and carried Powers by litter to the highway where he was taken by Flight for Life to St. Anthony's Hospital in Denver. Global Rescue was also contacted. Powers sustained substantial internal injuries, broken C6, C7, T6 and L1 vertebrae, thirteen broken ribs and a broken left humerus as a result of the fall.

Analysis

As the more experienced climber, it was my responsibility to acknowledge my belayer's experience level and give her more information before leaving the ground, especially at such a noisy location. Wood reported that in her past experiences, it was common practice for her climbing partners to rappel from the bolt anchor. "I couldn't see Phil, and the road and river noise made hearing difficult as well. When Phil climbed down to place the directional, it felt to me like he was pulling up the rope he would need to rappel on. The combination of signals I was receiving led me to believe he wanted to be taken off belay so that he could rappel."

Because Wood was not able to see or clearly hear Powers as he was climbing, failure to discuss what Powers planned to do when he reached the anchors contributed to the confusion that caused this accident. Clearer communication and planning can prevent accidents like this from happening to climbers of all skill levels and experience. That said, taking a climber off belay is a serious decision that should only be made when there is complete clarity about the situation. (Source: Phil Powers)

FALL ON ROCK, ROCKFALL
Colorado, Poudre Canyon

Late in the day on May 23 a female climber (31) was injured when she was struck by a rock and fell about 20 feet in Poudre Canyon, which is northwest of Fort Collins. She suffered a broken ankle, a crushing injury to her hand, and head lacerations. She was wearing a helmet.

She was transported to Poudre Valley Hospital after an hours-long rescue hampered by rugged terrain and darkness. (Source: 9news.com)

Analysis

Rockfall is a common objective hazard in many areas. Be prepared by becoming aware of those areas where it is common and develop the appropriate tactics to avoid being struck by rock fall. (Source: Aram Attarian)

FALL ON ROCK, PROTECTION PULLED OUT, NO HARD HAT
Colorado, Boulder Canyon, Practice Rock

Reid Pletcher (22), and I (Mali Noyes) were climbing together on May 26. This was going to be our last climb of the day. He was leading the climb, placing gear as he ascended. When he was about 20-30 feet up the wall, he unexpectedly fell. At this point, he had four trad pieces in, but the top two pulled out. He landed on the rock ledge next to me. Because the ledge is downward sloping, I had to keep Reid on belay to keep him from sliding off the ledge. So I called for help.

For the minute or two that I waited for help, I could see Reid spitting and slowly moving his arms and legs. The four other climbers that were nearby were very helpful. We tried to calm him down and stabilize his head. He had a laceration on the back of his head and was bleeding a lot from his left ear. He was very confused and uncooperative. He kept on trying to stand up. While it was not ideal, he was most comfortable in the fetal position with his head in my lap. I applied pressure to the laceration on the back of his head and treated him the best I could for shock. While I was not next to him for the first one to two minutes after the fall, he was conscious and knew his name and my name the entire time. The Nederland Fire Department, Pridemark Paramedics, and Rocky Mountain Rescue safely removed Pletcher from the rock ledge and he was taken by helicopter to St. Anthony's Hospital where he was diagnosed with two skull fractures, brain contusions with a subdural hemorrhage and a wrist contusion. He is expected to make a full recovery after rehabilitation.

Analysis

Reid was not wearing a helmet. Wear a helmet! Helmets are designed to protect the climber's head by absorbing energy and protecting against penetration. The consequences of not wearing a climbing helmet and sustaining a head injury could lead to impaired motor skills and paralysis, memory loss, altered personality, speech difficulty, and other life - changing issues. (Source: Mali Noyes, mountainproject.com)

FALL ON ROCK – INCOMPLETE TIE-IN KNOT
Colorado, Eldorado Canyon State Park

On May 28, Colin Gregg (34) was top-roping the first pitch of C'est La Vie (5.9) on Redgarden Wall. He had difficulty at a crux about 30 feet off the starting belay ledge (which is about 25 feet above ground level) and partially hung on the rope. The belayer reported that a lot of slack suddenly came into the system. When he tried to take in the slack, he noticed that the rope had come untied from the climber's harness. Gregg could not clip into fixed gear in his vicinity and though he fought to stay on the rock, he fell. Somehow his fall stopped roughly at the level of the starting belay ledge, saving him from an additional 25-foot fall to ground level.

Greg was alert and oriented after the fall, but complained of lumbar back pain. He was evacuated and transported to a hospital by ambulance. It is unknown whether the victim's tie-in knot was too loose, unfinished, or tied incorrectly.

Analysis

Climbers should double-check themselves and each other: harness double-backed and tied in properly, knot in the end of the rope, belay rigged properly, and carabiner locked, etc. (Source: Steve Muehlhauser – Park Ranger, Eldorado State Park)

FALL ON ROCK, FAILURE TO FOLLOW ROUTE
Colorado, Clear Creek Canyon

Andy (28) and his partner Tamie (28) were climbing at Canal Zone during the evening of June 21. Andy had clipped the last bolt on Holiday Road (5.8) and was climbing to anchors on a slabby headwall with minimal holds. He was to the left of the bolt line when he slipped then fell. He most likely took a pendulum fall to the right, hitting his left ankle on a ledge below the final headwall. The left ankle was broken laterally towards the outside, suggesting that Andy was moving to the right when he hit the ledge. The ledge slopes upwards towards climber's left so it might have been closer to him than if he was more in line with the bolts.

Credit goes to Tamie, a petite woman (less than 100 pounds) who was anchored to a tree at the base of the climb and able to arrest Andy's fall. It doesn't appear she was lifted off the ground due to the fall, nor was she pulled tight on her anchor.

Analysis

Andy might have been better off staying closer to the bolt line than moving left in an attempt to find easier holds. A tighter belay might also have minimized the fall. But rope stretch and the climber being off-route may have contributed to the distance of the fall. (Source: Alan Robertson)

FALL ON ROCK – POOR COMMUNICATION
Colorado, Eldorado Canyon State Park, The Bastille

On July 9, Darrell Kangiser (25) lead the first pitch of The Bastille Crack (5.8). When he arrived at the anchor (~35 feet above the ground), his belayer (23) thought he saw the leader signal that he was off belay, so the belayer let go. The leader leaned back to be lowered and fell to the ground. Fortunately the rope was still running through the belayer's belay device and this provided some friction to slightly slow the leader's fall to the ground. The leader landed on his feet and reported low back pain. He was transported by ambulance to a hospital.

Analysis

Climbing partners should be clear on the intended course of action (belay from above, lower, rappel, etc.) before they start the climb and exercise clear communication at all times. (Source: Steve Muehlhauser – Park Ranger, Eldorado Canyon State Park)

(Editor's Note: See May 17 incident.)

FALL ON ROCK, CLIMBING ALONE, DARKNESS
Colorado, El Diente Peak

Joe Yearm (28) was descending El Diente Peak (14,159 feet) in the San Juan National Forest alone after dark on Saturday July 16 when he fell 20 feet into a snowfield and fractured his leg. Yearm spent the night in the snow until he began crawling Sunday morning. Two other climbers in the area discovered him, one of whom activated a personal locator beacon, alerting authorities to the GPS position. (Officials noted there is no cell phone coverage in the area.) The climbers administered first aid, using hiking poles and duct tape to splint the Yearm's leg.

A construction company working in the area suspended operations and provided a helicopter to help search. According to the San Miguel County Sheriff's Office, the pilot made a "toe-in landing" on a "very steep slope," allowing rescue workers to reach the group, about a half-mile southwest of El Diente's summit. Rescuers said storm clouds were descending on the area and the weather was close to halting flight operations. Yearm was airlifted to the Telluride Airport and taken by ambulance to St. Mary's Hospital in Grand Junction, Colo. He was treated for a lower-leg fracture. (Source: axcentral.com)

Analysis

Solo climbing and mountaineering requires that the climber be prepared and have the ability to make the right decisions. Even the most experienced climbers can have an accident and be unable to extricate themselves from vertical terrain. The risk is increased if the injury occurs in difficult terrain and in deteriorating conditions. Climbers attempting any peak should leave an itinerary with someone who will monitor it; have the right equipment, clothing, and food in case they need to spend the night out; and have a reliable device to signal for help. (Source: Aram Attarian)

SLIP ON STEEP SNOW, CLIMBING ALONE, CLIMBING UNROPED, INADEQUATE EQUIPMENT/CLOTHING
Colorado, Rocky Mountain National Park (RMNP), Longs Peak

On July 22 at about 1300 hours a 68 year-old solo climber notified RMNP Dispatch that he had taken a 30-foot fall on steep snow at the junction of Lambslide Couloir and Broadway and had injured his shoulder while self-arresting. He was able to make it to a rock ledge on Broadway but was unable to continue or descend. He said that prior to the fall he noticed that his crampon was loose but that he thought he could make it to the ledge for readjustment.

Rangers responded and assisted him via simul-rappel and then out to the trailhead by rangers and horse.

Analysis

The climber's gear was made in the early '70s and included a long wood ice ax and crampons with leather straps that were difficult to adjust. In addition, the climber did not have sufficient bivouac gear. If rescue had not come quickly or inclement weather occurred the outcome may have been different.

Cell phone coverage is spotty at best in the mountains. The day before the climb, the man purchased a cell phone from a carrier that is known to have significantly better coverage in the area. Without the phone, it may have been days before he was located because he neglected to leave details of his trip with anyone.

Several weeks prior to this incident, this same climber was rescued by rangers after injuring his ankle in what was described as a "training" ascent of Mount Lady Washington. (Source: RMNP Search and Rescue)

FALL ON ROCK, LEDGE BREAKS BENEATH CLIMBER'S FEET
Colorado, Rocky Mountain National Park, Longs Peak

On Sunday August 28, Keith Brett (29) fell from the North Chimney while simul-climbing with his partner Matt. Their intention was to climb Pervertical Sanctuary (5.10d-5.11a). Here is how Keith described his incident:

Before light (probably around 5:15 a.m.), we were approximately 100 feet from Broadway Ledge. I was above and there were three to four pieces of gear between my partner and me. I was off route for a moment, then down climbed, got back on route and started moving up again. While standing on what I thought to be a stable ledge (six to eight inches wide) for a few seconds, it suddenly released. I was about 30 feet above my last piece of gear. I took about a 25-foot free-fall before hitting a ledge and tumbled for the remainder of the fall until the rope eventually caught me. No gear pulled. The fall was 60-70 feet total. I didn't lose consciousness. I was wearing a helmet.

My partner was able to eventually climb up to the ledge to assist me. A group of friends who were lower in the North Chimney joined us and helped lower me out of the chimneys and get me back to our bivy cave at the top of Mill's Glacier where we waited for assistance. Rangers met our group and provided medical care. I was flown off Mills Glacier via medical helicopter and taken to Denver.

Injuries I sustained were: a left wrist fracture in two places, two broken ribs, a punctured left lung, and some cuts and deep bruises with a few requiring stitches. The lung and breathing were the major issues. Thanks to everyone who helped me out during this incident including the RMNP rangers (top notch), friends and everyone else who was around. This really shows how strong and what amazing people make up the climbing community. Hope to be back at it soon! (Source: Keith Brett)

Analysis

Even though the North Chimney is rated 5.6, loose, wet rock, difficult route finding and lack of protection can potentially make this approach route to the Diamond the crux of the day. Objective hazards such as rockfall, long run-outs, and difficult route finding should be anticipated on a route such as this. The climbing party did an excellent job of self-rescuing down to Mills Glacier. If the SAR team needed to climb and then perform a technical lower, the rescue would have likely extended late into the night, requiring the patient to overnight on Mills Glacier. (Source: RMNP Search and Rescue)

STRANDED - INADEQUATE EQUIPMENT
Colorado, Eldorado Canyon State Park

On September 3,, a male (29) and female (30) climbed The Yellow Spur (5.9/5.10) on Redgarden Wall. When the climbers topped-out, they asked the party just ahead of them (the second party of climbers) if they would wait so they all could descend together, since the climbers were not familiar with the descent. The second party of climbers declined to wait since it was getting dark and they did not have headlamps. When the second party of climbers returned to the parking lot, they reported that the other party of climbers might have difficulty descending in the dark. Rangers heard shouting in the direction of the top of The Yellow Spur but could not make out what was being said. Rocky Mountain Rescue Group responded, made contact with the stranded climbers at about midnight, and escorted them down to the parking lot by about 1:00 a.m. AM.

Analysis

Be prepared. Climbs often take longer than anticipated. Bring headlamps, light jacket, etc. (Source: Steve Muehlhauser – Park Ranger, Eldorado Canyon State Park)

FALL ON ROCK, INADEQUATE PROTECTION, UNABLE TO COMMUNICATE WITH PARTNER
Colorado, Buena Vista Crags

On September 26, I was approximately 18 feet up a dihedral that was maybe 22 feet tall, about to make the crux move on a route (name unknown, left of Pump Station at Buena Vista crags). I had relatively good gear with my last piece being maybe seven feet below me, when my right foot blew. I immediately lost it and came off. As I fell I saw the rope coiling through the gear, hoping it would hold, as the last piece was a small Mastercam. It held, but only really caught me about a foot above the ledge/slab that the dihedral started out of. I crashed my entire weight onto my right foot, and in an effort to crumple as much as possible, I slid backwards a ways down the slab. I immediately heard/felt the explosion in my ankle and began yelling down to my belayer to prepare to lower me. The impact had blown my shoe off my foot, so I gathered myself and hopped over the pillar that made up the first half of the route and lowered with my broken and severely deformed ankle away form the wall. I got to the ground and crab-crawled a short distance to flat ground while my buddy assessed me.

Surprisingly I wasn't injured anywhere else. I drank water for a little bit while my belayer searched for help to get me out. Fortunately we were only a hundred yards from my truck so I crab crawled back to it while he was gone searching, just to give myself something to do instead of thinking about the ankle. After an hour and a half drive to Salida, I got into the ER, where I was diagnosed with a fractured talus.

Analysis

I think the accident happened for a few reasons. 1) I had gotten used to running it out and making it on similar terrain. Because of this attitude, I wasn't fully committed and didn't place additional gear. 2) I lost both visual and audible contact with my belayer during the climb and without that you can't properly belay. My guess is there was more slack in the system because of the wandering nature of the route, but also my belayer knows I hate being short roped. So he couldn't tell, and I couldn't tell him I was in a bad place to be given too much slack. 3) I should have down climbed and re-assessed the moves instead of going through expecting that, as usual, I would stick when in fact I was on incredibly dense/slick granite. Again I didn't treat it with the respect it deserved and I got spanked. (Source: Brice Harris from a post on mountainproject.com)

STRANDED, UNFAMILIAR WITH DESCENT
Colorado, Eldorado Canyon State Park

On October 15, rescuers were notified that two overdue climbers, Nicholas Kainrath (22) and Bryan Karban (23), were stranded on a rock climb in the Canyon. A search was started and the climbers were located. The two advised members of Rocky Mountain Rescue that they did not know how to get down from their current position. They were guided down by the rescuers. (Source: Boulder County Sheriffs Department)

Analysis
Climbers are encouraged to familiarize themselves with traditional self-rescue techniques, carry a route topo, and become familiar with descent routes to prevent situations like this from occurring. (Source: A. Attarian)

STRANDED, DARKNESS, POOR PLANNING
Colorado, Boulder Canyon, Castle Rock

On October 24, Gary Hansen (54) and his daughter Kate (17) became stranded on Castle Rock on a ledge 200 feet up the East Face after dark as they attempted to rappel. A rescue climber from the Rocky Mountain Rescue Group climbed over Castle Rock and descended to the stranded climbers. Each of them was then lowered to the ground, and they were both safely on the ground at 10:30 p.m.

Analysis
While these were experienced climbers, the situation they found themselves in was largely attributable to a lack of familiarity with the area, and not allowing enough time for their climb to the summit. Once on the summit after dark, they chose a descent route for which they were not properly equipped. However, they then made the right decision to call for help rather than attempt to climb further in the dark in an unfamiliar area. (Source: Boulder County Sheriff's Office)

STRANDED, CLIMBING ALONE, FREE SOLO CLIMBING, OFF ROUTE, INADEQUATE EQUIPMENT
Colorado, First Flatiron

Late in the afternoon on December 10 Xavier Rojas (20) became stranded while free soloing the Direct (Standard) East Face (5.6), a six-pitch route on the First Flatiron. According to authorities, Rojas was about 500 feet up the face when the temperature started falling and the rock iced up. In order to avoid the ice, Rojas went off route until he reached a spot where he could not continue. He was wearing a sweatshirt and climbing pants, and he had a headlamp. He used his cellphone to call 911 and communicate with rescuers, who arrived at the Flatiron by 6:25 p.m. and were able to call to Rojas. He was cold, but not injured.

To reach Rojas, rescuers used ice-climbing gear to get to a point about 180 feet above him, reaching him at 7:50 p.m. They provided him with extra clothing, then hauled Rojas up the 180 feet to the rescue point. A short rappel brought Rojas to the ground. He and his rescuers hiked out to the trailhead by 9:00 p.m. (Source: The Denverchannel.com)

Analysis

When soloing long routes, consideration should always be given to one's skill level, time of day, weather and rock conditions, and clothing and equipment needs before leaving the ground. Cell phone and proximity to rescue helped in this case. (Source: Aram Attarian)

FALL ON ROCK, RAPPEL ERROR – NO KNOT ON ROPE END, NO HARD HAT, INEXPERIENCE
Colorado, Eldorado Canyon State Park

During the afternoon of December 17, Dalton Jones (18) and his female partner (17) were climbing Rewritten (5.7), a six-pitch climb on the Redgarden Wall. Jones successfully led the first pitch, established an anchor, and began belaying his partner. Approximately halfway through the climb, she began to have some difficulty. At this point he lowered her to the base of the climb and told her to stay tied in.

To descend, he set his rope on an anchor and rappelled on the single, free strand of rope, using his partner as the lower anchor and the upper anchor as a redirect. He neglected to check the length of his rappel strand and to tie a knot in the end. As a result, he rappelled off the end, falling about 30 feet. He landed approximately two feet from his partner. He was not wearing a helmet and suffered a two-inch laceration to the back of his head and a fractured left femur.

The first rescuer reached Jones at 1:32 p.m. Jones complained of head pain and severe upper leg pain but was alert and oriented. He was packaged onto a litter for evacuation at approximately 2:44 p.m. and a Flight for Life chopper was requested. Rescuers then evacuated Jones down the hill on a belayed litter to the creek. A Tyrolean traverse was utilized crossing the river. At 3:35 p.m., Jones was placed into an ambulance for transport to the waiting Flight for Life chopper.

Analysis

Why didn't Jones' partner see what was about to happen? Inexperience. The dangling free end that he was about to rappel was clearly visible from his position and would have been visible to her as well.

A rappel backup might have prevented this accident. The two

primary methods of backup for preventing mistakes or loss of control include tying a knot on the end of the rope or using a Prusik or other friction knot attached to the rappel rope and the climber's harness. Better communication between Jones and his partner (or vice versa) may also have prevented this accident, especially since his partner was inexperienced. (Source: Bill May and Aram Attarian)

FALL ON ROCK, BELAYER TAKES HAND OFF ROPE
Kentucky, Red River Gorge

On Friday, March 4, I (name and age not on post) was climbing at The Motherlode on a route called Kick Me in the Jimmie (5.12) when I fell late in the day. The last fall of the last climb of the day should have been a routine, clean ~12-foot leader fall onto the fifth bolt. After the expected catch passed, it became clear that my belayer didn't have control of the rope. I fell about 35 feet to the ground.

I remember bracing myself for impact, hitting the ground, and letting everyone know that I was okay about one second after I hit. I injured my ankle and my butt hurt. I was able to walk out just fine. The belayer had rope burns on the wrist of his non-brake hand.

Analysis

My belayer had been climbing for ten years and I'd been climbing with him for just over a year. He was belaying with a tube-style device similar to a Wild Country VC Pro.

From what we could gather, he took his brake hand off the rope for a split second while moving into a better position to catch the fall. Once he realized his hand wouldn't be able to get the rope, he tried compressing it by leaning forward and just pressing his forearms onto the device/rope and in the process received rope burns on his forearm.

Relying on the belayer now is mentally difficult for me. I tried climbing on the following Sunday and Monday. Even being lowered is terrifying if I start to accelerate even a little bit. If this accident had been with an inexperienced belayer, I could have blamed myself, finding fault with trusting a "beginner" belayer. But now, considering that someone with ten years of experience dropped me, I have gotten in the mindset of, "How can I really trust anyone?" My plan is to go to the gym and practice taking larger and larger falls until I can get back to my old self. Please stay alert while you're belaying. It's your only job. (Source: Edited from a post on rockclimbing.com)

FALL ON ROCK, POOR COMMUNICATION, INADEQUATE BELAY – DISTRACTED
Kentucky, Red River Gorge, Muir Valley

On March 21, I took a lead fall, landing at the base of the climb Suppress the Rage (5.12a) located at the Sunny Side. I was at the second-to-last bolt when I decided to rest before making the last hard move. I must admit that I started climbing kind of suddenly, maybe surprising my belayer. Anyway, when I was less than one meter above the bolt I fell off. Before I had time to realize what was happening, I found myself screaming and hitting the ground with my right leg and then my butt. Fortunately the rope got tight at the very last second, so I didn't fully impact the ground. But still, I broke my pelvis and two vertebrae.

Analysis

Here is why I think this happened. First of all, my belayer got distracted as soon as I decided to rest for a few seconds. I saw him talking with people while I started falling. Second, there was too much slack in the rope, because it doesn't make sense to take a 12-meter fall, when you're only one meter above the bolt. Third, he told me that, as soon as he realized I was falling, he grabbed the rope above and below the Grigri, compromising its activation.

The moral is to pay attention to what you are doing. Always confirm that your belayer knows how to belay properly. The Grigri can be a deceiving belay device to use for the inexperienced. Some think it works by itself and don't pay attention to how it functions in the correct way!

I've been climbing for more than ten years and consider myself to be experienced. This was the first time climbing with this person, so we didn't know each other well enough, and there was probably lack of communication. It wouldn't happen to me with my usual climbing mates. (Source: Edited from a report by Francesco Peci)

FALL ON ROCK, PROTECTION PULLED OUT, INADEQUATE PROTECTION
Kentucky, Red River Gorge, Muir Valley

On April 22, a male climber (40) was nearing the top of a short dihedral on a trad route called "Short and Sweet" (5.7), located at the Practice Wall. He took a lead fall, causing his upper protection pieces to pop out, causing him to hit the ground. He sustained a crushed vertebra. He was carefully packaged onto a spine board, placed in a litter, and delivered to an awaiting helicopter.

Analysis

This accident was caused by tenuously placed gear. The climber commented that he should have put in more pieces. (Source: Rick Weber)

FALL ON ROCK, INEXPERIENCE, FAILED TO THREAD ROPE THROUGH ANCHORS
Kentucky, Red River Gorge, Muir Valley

A male climber (31) fell from the top anchors of Rat Stew (5.10a). He landed two feet from his belayer after free falling approximately 75 feet.

Moments after he decked, another climber who witnessed the fall ran to the nearest emergency call station and radioed for help. A helicopter was requested and landed at a nearby Landing Zone and awaited delivery of the patient. He was treated, packaged, and transported to the University of Kentucky Medical Trauma Center.

Analysis

The climber was cleaning the anchors and members of his party were expecting him to rappel when he fell. It was his first or second time cleaning anchors in an outdoor climbing environment. He failed to thread his rope through the top anchor rings and when he unclipped his tether, there was nothing to keep him from free falling to the ground. He has no recollection of climbing that day so he cannot provide any information as to why he failed to clean correctly.

Even though he suffered horrific massive internal injuries and traumatic brain injury, he survived the fall. He spent months in rehabilitation and physical therapy and has made a substantial recovery. (Source: Rick Weber)

FALL ON ROCK – RAPPEL ERROR, UNEVEN ROPES, NO KNOT ON ROPE END, DISTRACTION

Kentucky, Red River Gorge, Muir Valley

On July 16, a male climber (22) fell as he descended from the top anchors on the sport route Plate Tectonics (5.9). After cleaning the top anchors, he descended on a double-rope rappel. Unfortunately, one end of his rope did not reach the ground. As a result, he rappelled off the end of his rope from a height of approximately 50 feet and impacted the ground close to members of his party.

Eight members of the Muir Valley Rescue Group responded within five minutes. The patient was semi-conscious and in intense pain, and exhibiting signs and symptoms of hypovolemic shock and a fractured pelvis. A helicopter was called in and arrived quickly. The patient was treated and transported to the University of Kentucky Medical Trauma Center where he was treated for a shattered pelvis, dislocated elbow, and significant blood loss.

Analysis

There were two classic errors and one related problem here.

First, the climber did not make sure that both ends of his rope were on the ground before rigging his rappel device. Second, he did not tie a knot in the end of this rope, which would have prevented him from rappelling off the end.

The woman who had belayed him did not remain attentive until her climber was back on the ground. Had she not been distracted by other climbers in the area, she may have noticed that one strand of the rappel rope had not reached the ground and could have let her partner know that fact. (Source: Rick Weber)

(Editor's Note: The Muir Valley Climbing and Nature Preserve is one of the

more popular climbing areas in the Eastern U.S. with more than 30,000 visitors in 2011. Muir's seven miles of cliff line attract climbers from all over the world to its 350+ sport and trad routes. Rick and Liz Weber founded Muir in 2004 when it was opened at no charge to the public.)

FALL ON ROCK, PROTECTION PULLED OUT - POORLY PLACED, EXCEEDING ABILITIES, NO HARD HAT
Kentucky, Red River Gorge

On October 22, my group and I (Gram Parker – 40) were climbing in the Long Wall area of Red River Gorge attempting Rock Wars (5.10a, trad). I was approximately 60 feet up when I became unsure of my feet. Deciding I needed a rest, I asked for a "take" a few feet above the last piece I had clipped. Feeling uncomfortable about trying to down climb the layback finger crack and thinking of the climb in more of a sport lead mentality, I let go, trusting that my belayer had pulled in enough slack and therefore I wouldn't fall that far below it.

I felt the piece catch, and then I started to fall again. My only thoughts were, "Okay, the piece came out, maybe the next one will hold. Nope. Maybe the third." And then I was on the ground, lying on my back. I looked up and said, "I'm okay! I'm okay!" This was really only meant to convey that I was conscious, and that I hadn't hit my head or injured my neck.

Everyone rushed to my side, asking if I was hurt and telling me not to move. I wasn't planning on it, at least not until I could get a better idea of what had happened and what, if any, injuries I had sustained. In the midst of responding, the pain in my ankle spiked and I could tell my back hurt in more than a few places.

Luckily, a member of a group climbing nearby was an ICU doctor and was able to check me out before the EMTs arrived. He also gave me some ibuprofen to help with the pain. The first EMT on the scene was part of the helicopter crew that would take me to the University of Kentucky's ER. He ran an IV and administered pain medications through it. He also put me in a neck brace, just in case. Once the team arrived, I was placed on a backboard, strapped down, and placed in a basket and carried for three hours in darkness to an ambulance that transported me to a waiting helicopter.

Analysis

That's the story of what happened. The story of how it happened is another thing entirely. My friend, Rodney, decided he wanted to lead Rock Wars. So, he did. His experience with trad climbing was not extensive. His placements were poor. I could see this as he climbed the route, though I only noted that he didn't place gear with respect to the direction of load. I should've said something. After his climb, I did ask the most experienced member of our group about his placements, and my suspicions were confirmed.

Our friend, J, seconded the climb, but left the gear in place. I decided to lead it on the already placed gear, thinking that a 5.10a shouldn't be too much of a problem for me.

As I climbed, I only placed a single piece of gear. Rodney had placed a piece very deep, and it was difficult to remove (so) I replaced it. I should have been doing the same for all the other pre-placed pieces, removing each and placing them deeper in the crack. They were also a size too small, so the cams were too flared. I didn't have the proper gear or knowledge to fix the placements.

As I let go after asking for a take—with the mindset of a sport climber (my fifth mistake), the piece twisted, locked up, and tore away a chunk of rock as it tried to hold. The two pieces below also twisted and came out, though they didn't take as much rock with them. Final mistake: I wasn't wearing my helmet.

The luck I had that day bore these lessons into me like a laser:

• Wear a helmet! I don't care what you think of yourself or your self-image. You can fall. And you can hit your head. Do it.

• What you climb on sport lead doesn't translate to trad. Trad climbing is a different level of climbing that takes years to feel comfortable and even more to master.

• Know what you're doing. If you're climbing at your limit on trad, you had better know exactly what you're doing or you will pay the consequences. (Source: Gram Parker)

FALL ON ROCK, CLIMBING ALONE, FAILURE TO MAINTAIN CONTROL OF ROPE, UNFAMILIAR WITH DEVICE, NO BACK-UP, FATIGUE
Nevada, Red Rock Canyon NCA, Tunnel Vision

On February 4, a male climber had been rope soloing the 5.9 bolted first pitch variation to Tunnel Vision when he decided to retreat at the fourth bolt due to the pitch being harder then anticipated. When rappelling, he experienced difficulty with the device repeatedly "locking" and was trying to find a position on the lowering handle that would cause the rope to lower with less drag. (He was using a fairly new 60mx10.2 rope.)

He had placed the handle in the full open locked position and was trying to find a position in the handle range that he had used before to get a smooth descent. At some point, he took his hand off the brake side of the rope and began to use both hands to try and adjust the handle. There was no backup in place.

The device unlocked abruptly in mid range (between the locked open and closed handle positions) and the climber went into free fall of about 25 feet. He managed to grab the brake side of the rope, causing rope burns to his hand. The device then locked but during dynamic stretch of the rope, he impacted the ground feet first. He injured both ankles. His left ankle was immediately unusable and the right ankle was also damaged to the extent that he could not place any weight on it a short time later. He was extremely fortunate to be in a rare position within Red Rock that had cell coverage and that he had chosen to bring his phone with him.

He waited about an hour before initiating rescue. The responding BLM ranger reached him about an hour later and after assessing the situation elected for a helicopter extraction. After assessment by EMT personnel, the climber chose to refuse further treatment and was picked up at the location by a friend. (The injuries turned out to be minor.)

Analysis

The primary cause of the accident was that the climber failed to maintain control of the rope and utilize a backup. A backup should always be used when rappelling, especially when soloing. In addition, the climber's hand should not have been off of the brake side of the rope.

Other factors that contributed to this incident:

• Misjudgment of the route. The route was close to the climber's maximum lead capability under normal circumstances.

• The self-arrest device in use was an Edelrid Eddy and the climber had tried it only twice before.

• Exhaustion. The climber had considered retreating earlier in the climb but continued on. He was suffering both from physical stress and mental stress due to the grade of the route and climbing alone. (Source: Edited from a post on mountainproject.com by Travis Spalding, one of his climbing partners – hence no name and no age, we assume.)

FALL ON ROCK, INADEQAUTE PROTECTION
Nevada, Red Rock Canyon NCA, Pine Creek Canyon

On March 12, around 1:00 p.m., there was a serious leader fall on the lower section of the third pitch (the long 5.8 corner) of the route Dark Shadows on the Mescalito Formation in the Pine Creek Canyon area. It seems that the leader was about 30 feet above the belay ledge with insufficient protection and slipped while trying to place gear. He dropped the gear and landed on the small ledge just above the belay right-side down. It does not appear that any gear failed.

There was one party above and one party below on the route. I was anchored just right of the Dark Shadows belay ledge at the anchor of Slot Machine (instead of rappelling to the Dark Shadows anchors). I saw about the last five feet of the fall. It was extremely disturbing.

A person in the party above was a doctor and one person below was a nurse. Those two parties worked tirelessly to stabilize the injured climber and set up anchors needed to bring up rescue personnel. It took about two hours for the first rescuer to arrive, as the narrow canyon and trees made it difficult for the helicopter to do much. I think they were able to drop off people and gear bit by bit at about the halfway point on the trail. (I waited at the Slot Machine anchor with a partner—until it was confirmed that we would not be needed for assistance immediately—and watched the helicopter make several passes.

After another hour or so and after about three more SAR personnel arrived, they built a setup of anchors and pulleys using trees and boulders on the ground. Luckily we had extra ropes and plenty of people on the ground to assist with hauling a rescuer and litter up to the ledge. When the climber was in the litter, he was lowered with the rescuer and several of us helped pull the litter away from the water and carried it up to a point where the helicopter could drop a line and evacuate the patient by air. From fall to helicopter lift, the whole event took about eight hours.

I was told that the injuries included fractured leg and vertebrae with likely paralysis as a result. (Source: Edited from a post on mountainproject.com by Joseph Stover)

FALL ON ROCK, MISCOMMUNICATION
Nevada, Red Rock Canyon NCA, The Gallery

In late November, this incident arose from belayer error and miscommunication. The climber's belayer was deaf, while the climber could hear. They had some form of sign language while climbing. When she fell, her belayer's anchor was clipped and the rope was running through the belayer's ATC. (This I know because I later watched people remove the gear.)

People quickly responded and called 911. A former EMT/Paramedic supported her head while others kept her comfortable and warm. She was conscious, able to wiggle her toes, and could sense pressure on her feet.

Some friends of mine ran to the road to guide the EMS team to the crag, most of whom were extremely out of shape and took a longer than usual time to arrive. They further helped stabilize her and put her on a body board. A helicopter was called in and 90 minutes after the fall, she was short hauled to the road and put in an ambulance.

Through friends and acquaintances in common in the Bay Area, I've heard that she suffered lower vertebrae fractures and a potential ankle injury. (Source: Edited from a post on mountainproject.com by "Owie")

STRANDED
Nevada, Red Rock Canyon NCA, Black Velvet Canyon - Dream of Wild Turkeys

On November 26, two females became stuck between second and the top of the third pitch on Dream of Wild Turkeys (5.10a). They were stranded because their rope had lodged itself in a crack, making it unusable.

Pilots, officers, and MR Volunteers attempted to access the victims on Saturday night, but due to winds, terrain, and other factors, the decision to leave them on a ledge/crack was ultimately made in order to complete the rescue in a safer and more efficient manner on Sunday. Before leaving for the night, one officer was dropped off at the base of the cliff where voice contact was made with the climbers. It was confirmed that they were prepared to spend the remainder of the night in their current location.

Once technical systems were set up, one rescuer was lowered to the climbers. Upon arrival, the rescuer determined that both were medically stable. The rescuer was then lowered to the location where the rope had lodged. He was unable to free the rope but was able to cut it in such a manner that a portion of it could still be used. The rescuer was then raised back to the climbers where he helped them rappel to the valley floor. Once all members had reached the ground, the officer and climbers hiked out of the canyon. (Source: Edited from a post by the Las Vegas Metropolitan Police Dept. SAR Unit on lvmpdsas.blogspot)

AVALANCHE – TRIGGERED BY CLIMBER
New Hampshire, Mount Washington, Pinnacle Gully

On March 10 shortly after 10:30 a.m., a solo ice climber (31) fell approximately 1,150 feet after triggering an avalanche in Pinnacle Gully. The avalanche deposited him at the bottom of the area known as the "Fan" about 50 feet below the debris pile. He sustained significant injuries but was able to call 911 from his cell phone to alert authorities of the accident. USFS Snow Rangers were notified of the accident by the Androscoggin Ranger District and arrived on scene with rescue equipment around 11:15 a.m. After the patient's injuries were stabilized (possible fractured femur and noted—but not immediately treated—an angulated wrist and superficial facial contusions and abrasions) were stabilized, he was packaged into a rescue sled and transported behind a snowmobile to an ambulance waiting at the Pinkham Notch Visitor Center.

Analysis

The avalanche danger for Pinnacle Gully this day was listed as "Considerable", based on new snow being blown in on southerly winds around 40-50mph. Between 7.3" and 8.0" of new snow was recorded from the storm before it changed over to rain on Friday. It is unclear how much snow had fallen at the time of the avalanche, but we estimate about four inches. The avalanche was triggered in new snow sitting on top of a rain crust and was classified as D2R3. (Source: mountwashingtonavalanchecenter.org)

FALL ON SNOW – UNABLE TO SELF-ARREST, FAULTY USE OF CRAMPONS
New Hampshire, Mount Washington, Lion Head

On April 4, one member of a group was descending the Lion Head Winter Route control of his glissade. He slid an unknown length, impacted trees along the way, and came to rest wedged between two trees just above the first steep pitch on the route. The party was able to reach 911 via cell phone. Local caretakers from the AMC also heard their voices while skiing and went over to assist.

Due to the unfortunate location where he came to rest, stabilization and extrication was difficult and took longer than usual for accidents in this area. The patient was eventually packaged on a backboard in a rescue litter, which was lowered by rope through the steep sections of trail. He was loaded into the USFS snowcat and transferred to an ambulance at Pinkham Notch Visitor Center. The approximate time from injury to when he was transferred to the ambulance was four to five hours.

Analysis

We would like to remind everyone that glissading while wearing crampons is a dangerous activity. Every year people are injured doing this. If you do want to glissade, we recommend removing your crampons first. The Lion Head Winter Route is steep. It requires the ability to self-arrest. (Source: mountwashingtonavalanchecenter.org)

FALL ON ROCK
New Hampshire, Cathedral Ledge, Recompense

On June 18, Mark Gallagher (48) was climbing Recompense when he fell, hit a ledge, and suffered a compound fracture of his lower left leg. Gallagher said he had climbed Recompense several times before and he knew that he was heading into the most difficult moves on the climb. Following the fall, he was hanging from a rope 120 feet below the top of the cliff and 250 feet above the ground, just a couple feet away from his partner. "He lowered me down to him, pulled me over, and anchored me back into the belay."

Gallagher's partner pulled their cell phone. The call came into the Conway police dispatch center at 1:46 p.m., but rescuers were already on their way. Members of Mountain Rescue Service were nearby when Gallagher fell. They knew something was wrong even before they heard Gallagher yell.

Bayard Russell and Sam Bendroth, who have been on expeditions from Alaska to Patagonia, hopped into a car with two other climbers,

Freddie Wilkinson, another MRS member and a professional climber, and Mark Richey, former American Alpine Club president, and drove to the top of the cliff to begin a rescue. Gallagher couldn't have hoped for a better team.

"They were down to me in no time," Gallagher said. They brought a makeshift splint with them and stabilized his leg. They were able to apply direct pressure and stop the bleeding. "Then it was just kind of hurry up and wait."

MRS team leader Joe Lentini and US Forest Service ranger Jeff Lane went down with the litter to help load and raise Gallagher. Lentini described it as "textbook smooth," which was important because any movement hurt Gallagher. When the litter crested the top of the cliff an ambulance was waiting. Rescuers carried the litter to the road and Gallagher was rushed to Memorial Hospital.

"It's nice to have world-class climbers in our rescue community," said Sgt. Brian Abrams, of the state Fish and Game Department. (Source: Edited from an article in the Conway Daily Sun by Erik Eisele)

FALL ON ROCK – ASCENDER THREADED INCORRECTLY, DEHYDRATION
New Hampshire, Cathedral Ledge, The Prow

On August 8, a climber (40s) from Center Conway survived a 100-foot fall at Cathedral Ledge.

The Prow ascends the nose directly below the fenced-in viewing area at the top of the cliff. It's renowned both as a free climb and as a popular aid climb.

The two climbers were there to do the route as an aid climb; both were familiar with that type of climbing. They got several rope-lengths up over the course of the day and were several hundred feet off the ground.

The victim's partner took between 45 minutes and an hour and a half to climb to the next stance where he anchored the rope. The victim was supposed to ascend the rope, cleaning any gear as he went, but according to Rick Wilcox, head of Mountain Rescue Service (MRS), "He apparently suffered dehydration." He was having trouble setting up his gear and he fumbled and dropped a crucial ascending device. Without it, he had to rely on a backup device with which he was unfamiliar. "The backup device didn't work, which he was counting on," his partner said. The victim was hanging in space when he disconnected himself from the anchor.

"That was the last thing tethering him to the line. He had a 50-foot loop under him, so he fell 100 feet," Wilcox said.

The rope caught him before he sailed to the ground below. Their rope, it turned out, had taken a beating in the fall. The sheath was singed for 30 or 40 feet. More than half of it was either burned or shredded.

Local climber, guide, and MRS member, Jim Surette rappelled down to the victim, who was once again anchored high on the cliff, but whose condition was quickly getting worse. He wasn't losing consciousness, Surette said, but he was unable to pick himself up. "He didn't want a rescue, but he didn't want to get up."

Surette lowered him to the ground and put in a call for a rescue litter and a backboard, which Wilcox and other team members brought up to the base of the cliff. "We then lowered him straight through the woods 200 feet," Wilcox said. When ambulance personnel arrived, they put in an IV, and the rescue team continued the carryout. (Source: Edited from an article in the Conway Daily Sun by Erik Eisele)

Analysis

The device is a CAMP lift ascender. Very interesting... I was truly surprised in looking at it with my partner. We both agree that it is entirely possible and quite easy to thread incorrectly resulting in zero friction. The CAMP device can be oriented correctly in your hand and on the rope and even look correct, but still not be. Not at all (what) I expected. The Grigri and Mini-Traxion are far more visually user friendly (and are) not impossible, but far less likely, to be improperly installed. With all that said, I suppose it is always possible I installed it correctly, but on my tie-in side of the rope. A difficult proposition to admit. I only say this because the wear on the devise negligible. (Source: The victim, who wishes to remain anonymous)

RAPPEL ERROR – UNEVEN ROPES, FALL ON ROCK
New York, Shawangunks

On May 21, I met my friend Dana B. in the West Trapps lot for a day of climbing in the Gunks. I've been climbing for over 15 years and have climbed all over the country; I've lead honest 5.10 on gear, and done long routes. I started out on the first pitch of Middle Earth, and we rappelled from the tree above its first pitch. This uses the entire length of a 60m rope. Next, Dana climbed most of the route Snake and traversed left to the tree above Sente. Once I arrived at the tree, we talked about top-roping Sente but decided against it, as it looked like a short rainfall was moving in. We were only one rappel from the ground and it was a warm day, so we weren't worried about getting caught by rain.

We were using Dana's bi-pattern rope. I rigged the rope by lowering one end first. Dana let me know when I reached the pattern change, and then I tossed the other end. As often happens for that rappel, both ends were piled in a puddle on a ledge partway down. I use an ATC-type device to rappel and backed it up with a friction knot clipped to the leg loop of my harness – though I know that this does not protect me from unattended short ends. I am fairly sure the rope was even when I left the tree; I remember seeing both patterns of the two sides when I put myself on rappel. I stopped midway down to clear the rope from the ledge. I remember looking down and checking that the left side reached the ground, but I did not check the right side. I don't know why.

Less than a second later, I heard the dreadful 'click' of a rope end going through my device. Honestly, I have no idea how the ends got that uneven, but in the end, regardless of cause, it was my responsibility to make sure both ends hit the ground and I didn't. Just like forgetting to check a rearview mirror when changing lanes on a highway, it was a small mistake with big consequences.

When I heard the 'click', I yelled up to Dana, "I'm off the end!" That communication was purely reflexive, because if she weren't already watching, she'd see soon enough. I remember thinking that the ground seemed impossibly far away and thinking to myself, "Hmm... Wonder how this is going to go?" I fell somewhere between 30 and 40 feet.

I hit the ground first with my left foot. I felt a huge jolt of electricity up and down my spine when I hit and I remember thinking, "Uh, oh, I know what that is!" I bounced or rolled somehow. (My helmet later turned out to be cracked just above my ear.) As soon as I came to a stop, I took quick stock: Arms move. Legs move. Phew. Though I didn't feel pain, I knew something was very wrong with my left foot and I knew I didn't want to let it swell up in a climbing shoe, so I pulled that shoe off. I saw bone poking through skin on the inside of my heel and saw that the heel seemed oddly short. Somewhere in there I yelled for help, though I could already hear people yelling and knew they were coming. Then my back seized up and the pain kicked in. I crab-walked myself around a few feet in an attempt to get my back on a flat stable surface. In moments, there were probably a dozen people around me trying to keep me safe and comfortable.

The rescue was incredibly well organized and executed; I was very lucky, and have a lot of people to thank. There was a scary and painful litter carry (I apologize for everyone's ears. I know I was yelling from the pain), finally some morphine, a trip up the carriage road in the back of the pickup, an ambulance ride from the steel bridge to the field across from the Deli, a helicopter to Poughkeepsie, where I was scanned and x-rayed, and then another helicopter to Westchester, where I landed amongst world-class orthopedic trauma surgeons.

The damage: my left calcaneus was broken in several places, earning me seven screws and a plate. My L1 vertebra burst, and now I have a titanium cage in its center, and it's fused to the vertebrae above and below (T12 and L2). Very fortunately, I have no neurological deficit. The spine surgeon kept saying, "You were very, very lucky," because the burst vertebra came so close to pinching my spinal cord. I had a pleural effusion on the left side and was on a respirator for a day after the fusion surgery.

Analysis

For many climbing accidents, there's usually a bunch of post-hoc Analyses: What went wrong, and how can we avoid it? Especially for rappelling and lowering-off-the-end accidents, the idea that 'I just don't see how this happens' is pervasive.

As a neuroscientist, I feel particularly qualified to respond to 'I just don't see how this happens'. The answer is very simple, though it is also hard to confront and accept: Humans are fallible and our attention is imperfect. Human fallibility is why we tie knots in the ends of ropes, though that isn't always the answer. It's why auto-locking devices exist, though those sometimes cause new problems.

There are thousands of experiments and papers and such, accidents on all kinds of scales that demonstrate the imperfection of human attention. No one is exempt as appealing as it is to think that experts or experienced people might or should be. As 'R.G.' said, "Like many things in climbing, you can do it right thousands of times, screw it up once, and you're hosed." As for me, I get to live, walk, and climb again - and try harder to pay better attention. (Source: Edited from a report sent in by Julie Haas – 40)

FALLS ON ROCK (7), PROTECTION PULLED OUT (2), INADEQUATE PROTECTION, RAPPEL ERRORS (2), BELAY ERROR
New York, Mohonk Preserve, Shawangunks

Seven reports were submitted for 2011 (including the narrative above).

There was only one long fall. This male climber, who had over 20 years of experience, was rappelling after roped soloing when the rappel "system failed".

The average age of the climbers was 41 and the level of route difficulty was 5.8. The injuries included one sprains/strain, two lacerations, one dislocation, and two "unknowns" because the climbers refused care.

Four of the climbers were experienced, one had none of little experience and the others were unknown. (Source: From reports submitted by Mohonk Preserve)

FALL ON ROCK – FALL ON ROCK
North Carolina, Pilot Mountain State Park

On February 13, several others and I witnessed a long fall that resulted in a climber hitting the ground. I was climbing Foreign Trade Zone while a party of two was top-roping some variation of Bat Out of Hell (5.11). The climber reached the top of the route while I was about halfway up Foreign Trade Zone. I heard a "whoosh" and a loud thump and looked down to see the climber yell and bounce off the ground.

My belayer lowered me and we sent a couple people up the trail to call 911 and notify Park personnel. Meanwhile, the climber's partner, a couple others, and I tried to keep him still and attend to a small cut on the back of his head. He was alert, not injured, and otherwise seemed okay. Rangers and EMS arrived fairly quickly and checked him out. He was up and walking around and refused treatment. Both actually kept climbing.

His apparent lack of injury was pretty amazing to me. He had fallen from the top of the route, which I'd estimate at ~40 feet, and landed on his back/butt. His belayer had taken him off belay, assuming he was going to rappel, when he was, in fact, expecting to be lowered.

Analysis

This was a case of miscommunication between poorly trained, novice climbers. The climber never requested to be taken off belay. The belayer took him off and called, "Belay is off!" The climber never heard this and expected to be lowered. Anytime there is a belay change, especially at busy crags where it may also be hard to hear, always yell the person's name in the command. The anchor was inspected and found to have been constructed with the rope passing over a large ledge at the top of the route, thus creating a lot of rope drag. This configuration may have saved the climber from serious injury due to the friction in the system. It actually slowed down at least half of his fall. (Source: Edited from a post by C. Sproul on carolinaclimbers.org)

FALL ON ROCK, INADEQUATE BELAY, ROPE PULLS THROUGH BELAY DEVICE, NO HELMET

North Carolina, Looking Glass Rock

On March 23 around 1:50 p.m., a male climber (26) fell approximately 45 feet on the South Face of Looking Glass Rock. He had led Good Intentions (5.6) and traversed right to a set of rappel bolts over the climb Left Up, where he anchored to the bolts with the intent of being lowered. On his descent he was swinging over to remove gear.

At some point, the belayer stated that the rope end passed through the belay device and the climber fell to the ground. The climber suffered head and other injuries to the chest. EMS services were contacted and the patient was airlifted to Mission Hospital in Asheville, NC.

Analysis

The rope was tied to the climber and there was no apparent failure at the anchor point. There were still four pieces of gear in the rock that the rope was going through. The end of the rope on the belay side was approximately 25 feet in the air. The climber was wearing a helmet. The length of rope was unknown. The belay end of the rope did not have a back up knot. Typically a 60-meter rope will not be long enough to complete this maneuver.

Please remember to close the system while climbing. Either tie a back up knot on the end of the rope or tie in the belayer. This is measure can help prevent incidents. Also, please wear helmets while climbing. (Source: Patrick Weaver – Appalachian Mountain Institute)

FALL ON ROCK, PROTECTION PULLED OUT, CLIMBING ALONE

North Carolina, Looking Glass Rock, Invisible Airways

On the morning of April 12, Parker Kempf (21) was attempting an all-clean aid (solo) ascent of Invisible Airways (A2) on the north side of

Looking Glass Rock, his fourth time on the route. He had full big wall set- up including a portaledge, which was not deployed.

Parker was planning on fixing to the top of Invisible Airways (A1), descending, and attempting the Brain Wall the next day. Parker called Looking Glass Outfitters at 11:15 a.m. Parker was calm but in shock, coming in and out of periods of fright. He told me that he had "blown a cam hook trying to clip the bolt on the route and hit the

Waste Ledge". (The bolt is approximately 15 feet from the anchor on an 80-foot pitch). I asked him how he hit and if he was okay. He informed me that he had flipped upside down and landed on the back of his head and neck and that his helmet was destroyed. He was complaining of lower back pain. He was going to attempt to rappel down to the ground. I instructed him to stay on the ledge and that we would come out to get him. I didn't want him to rap if he had a head injury for fear that he would rig the rappel wrong and take a ground fall from the Waste Ledge. The ledge is 80 feet off the ground.

At this point there were three climbers in the shop hanging out and we confirmed the best course of action. The first phone call out of the shop was to Karsten Delap, who is on the Brevard Rescue Squad and is a local guide. He was out of the state and unavailable. The second call was to Marcus Webb in an attempt to organize a climbing team to go to the site. Marcus was unavailable. The third call was to Patrick Weaver of AMI for insight on the issue. Patrick gave instructions based on the above description and instructed us to call Parker back, ask a series of questions, and then re-ask those questions. Parker called the shop phone again and Patrick and I assessed the head injuries over the phone. Parker was doing better but still coming in and out of periods of fright. At this point Patrick and I decided to call 911, as his MOI was a possible 60-foot ledge fall on to his head. Joe Morchebacher was in the shop and was willing to help out as was the Black Diamond Rep Matt Ginley and his girlfriend, a former EMT. Joe M. gathered climbing gear and we drove out to the North Face parking lot following an ambulance.

Upon reaching the base of Looking Glass with paramedics and two members of the BRS, we ran into Nathan Brown and Frost Walker, two highly competent climbers. We briefed Nathan, who is a paramedic, and he volunteered to jug Parker's fixed rope to the Waste Ledge. After jugging the rope, Nathan took over, assessed Parker, and deemed no spinal injury but a probable tailbone injury. He then proceeded to slowly lower Parker to the paramedics on the ground. With the assistance from medics Parker limped out to the bottom of the boulder field where he boarded a BRS six-wheel ATV and was driven out the trailhead. Back at the parking lot, he refused treatment and then was taken by friends to Mission Hospital in Asheville for assessment and x-rays. (Source: Patrick Weaver, Appalachian Mountain Institute)

Analysis

While it is noted that Parker is a competent aid climber with several aid ascents on Looking glass and two ascents of El Capitan, he was, nevertheless, climbing alone. (Source: Jed Williamson)

FALL ON ROCK, RAPPEL ERROR
North Carolina, Rumbling Bald, Cereal Buttress

It was July 2, 10:30 a.m. I had met Joshua Haddock (29) only ten minutes before I heard his body impact the ground. Mike, Brian, his 15 year-old son Cole, and I had the Cereal Buttress to ourselves. It was still shaded and cool despite a forecast for the high 90s. Cole was leading Fruit Loops as a warm up. Two college-age guys walked by and we joked how we were surprised to see two other masochists climbing on a south-facing wall in July. They laughed, walked past us and started climbing a few routes away. A short while later Mike was top roping a climb, Cole was belaying, and Brian was taking pictures of Mike while on rappel.

I wandered over and started taking pictures of another climber, Lorenzo, as he cruised Frosted Flake (5.9). His belayer, JH, and I struck up a conversation about the area and its various access issues. After a few minutes I wandered back to my group. JH top roped their route. A few moments later we heard a frightening sound. Lorenzo called for help and I was at the scene within 30 seconds. JH lay crumpled at the base of the cliff beside a large embedded boulder.

Just five weeks earlier, I had taken a wilderness first aid class. I had hoped I would never have to use the knowledge I had gained but was suddenly grateful that I took the class. I yelled for my guys to get down now and call 911. Thankfully, Mike had a signal on his phone. I did a quick assessment. JH was in a fetal position. lying on his right side. He was alert and understood my questions. I realized within seconds we had a spinal issue because he could not move anything except his eyes. They were filled with fear but were still communicative. He could not feel me pinching him. His right thigh had an obvious deformity, and a look under his pant leg revealed an ugly compound fracture. There was little blood loss, though. Cole arrived next as he had lowered Mike to the ground. Brian wisely sent him, the nimblest among us, to run to the parking lot and lead the EMS crew to us once they arrived. The trail system to the Cereal Buttress is complicated and primitive. The last 200 yards involves boulder scrambling. The crew would have been greatly delayed without Cole's guidance.

Brian and Mike hurried to the scene once they were on the ground. At that time I noticed JH was turning ashen colored and his eyes no longer met mine. He had stopped breathing! Despite knowing he had a spinal injury, we had no choice but to straighten him out. We gently pulled his legs and torso away from the wall and got him on his back. Mike and Brian immediately began CPR. I elevated his good leg with a pack to get blood to his torso. I next began extracting him from the tangle of gear and rope around him. I cut him out of his harness and got the cams he was lying on out from under him. I got on the phone with 911 again and gave them an update to relay to the crew. An odd thing is that the call was answered by Polk County 911 rather than Rutherford County.

The next people on the scene were Ricky and Brittany, two climbers who had met Cole on his way down. Soon thereafter the Chimney Rock Fire Department's first responders showed up and we lead them to JH. It took roughly 45 minutes from the time the call went out until the first professionals arrived. Based on our remote location I believe that was a very fast response.

During the interim, JH "died" on us several times. Brian and Mike heroically brought JH's heartbeat back several times using CPR. We all yelled encouragement to JH throughout. I believe he was fighting as hard as he could on the inside.

Once the pro's arrived we gave them all the info we could and got out of the way. We rested, cried, and regrouped. We knew JH was in good hands but also realized the ordeal was far from over. Once the crew had JH on oxygen and inserted an IV, we still had to transport him. Mike, Ricky, Cole and I scouted and cleared a lower trail through the heavily forested talus at the base of the cliff. We met the backboard team and helped them disassemble the stretcher, which had a large rubber tire beneath it for trail travel. The wheel was worthless on the immediate terrain but was awesome once we were later back on a real trail. Ricky ran down the mountain several times to assist in bringing oxygen tanks and IV bags up from lower, slower crews.

By the time JH was ready for transport, there were probably 25 people at the scene, all eager and willing to do whatever it took to get this man safely down the mountain. It was a slow, laborious process carrying a stretcher down the treacherous mountainside, especially now that the temperature had risen to above 90 degrees. The volunteers and the professionals worked well together and we eventually got JH down to the wheel at the start of the better trail. Once the wheel was attached, we made excellent progress to a waiting ambulance that whisked JH off to a helicopter waiting in town that in turn took him to Memorial Mission Hospital in Asheville, where doctors found that Joshua had a broken neck. They were unable to fully revive him.

Analysis

Mike and I hiked the mile back uphill to investigate the scene and lug our gear out. JH's rappel device was still attached to the rope, but only by a single strand. Frosted Flake has fixed rings at the top. After threading his rope through the rings, JH apparently failed to ensure that both strands of rope were on the ground before he commenced his rappel. The ends and middle of his rope were marked at the factory. He also failed to "close the system", which means tie a knot in the ends of the rope. Had there been a knot at the end of the rope, it could not have slid through his rappel device and this accident would not have happened. The pictures I took of Lorenzo earlier show that he wore a helmet. JH did not. Mike and I photographed the evidence, then gathered it up and trudged out. (Source: Edited from a report by Sean Coburn)

(Editor's note: This is from a post on the Alpinist Web site: "Doctors were able to save Haddock's heart, lungs, liver, pancreas and kidneys for five different donors. Upon hearing that four men and one woman had received Joshua's organs, his mother, Pamela Haddock, found some comfort in that her son's death was able to give life to five others.")

FALL ON ROCK, OFF ROUTE
North Carolina, Stone Mountain

On October 21, we approached the base of Stone Mountain to climb U-Slot (5.7) and then the Great Arch (5.5). On our way to the climb, I noticed two men moving rather slowly across the boulder field at the base of The Block Route and U-Slot. One of the men yelled down to me and the two other climbers I was with saying, "We need help! I had a bad lead fall."

All three of us immediately dropped our packs and made our way up to the party of two, expecting the worst. When we got to them, I began asking them questions about the fall and his injuries. Dan (age unknown), the climber who had fallen, was standing and trying to scramble down between the rocks and trees with his older brother trying to assist him. Dan's brother stated that he was a paramedic and they just needed a couple of people to help get Dan down to the field so they could get their vehicle. Dan was able to walk but only with assistance from three of us, as he was unable to fully weight his left foot. Dan had major abrasions and rock burn from sliding down the slab of Stone Mountain. The majority of his injuries were on his left side, including his hand, wrist, arm, hip, ankle, and foot. When Dan's brother arrived with the truck he helped bandage his left arm before they packed up and began the drive out. We encouraged that they seek medical attention but are unsure if they did.

Analysis

As we talked with Dan we found out that he had been climbing for a long time and knew Stone Mountain and Block Route very well but was fairly new to leading.

This is a reminder that all climbers should know and understand their limits, especially on lead, and to make sure you pay attention to the route so you don't stray off, even if you have been on it before. (Source: David Crye)

FALL ON ROCK, NO HARD HAT
North Carolina, Crowder's Mountain State Park, Opinionated

On November 23, a male climber (23) fell while climbing Opinionated (5.9+) on the Red Wall at Crowder's Mountain State Park. According to reports, the climber was attempting to clip the third of six bolts when he fell. Witnesses noted that the climber flipped backwards, fell approximately eight feet, and struck his face against the cliff face, fracturing his nose, then suffered a seizure and lost consciousness. The climber and his belayer were not wearing helmets.

Analysis

This same spot has been the site of three previous falls, all with the same scenario – the inability of the climber to clip the third bolt. Climbers familiar with this route place a #2 C3 cam to protect the move after clipping the second bolt. (Source: Aram Attarian)

STRANDED, RAPPEL ERROR – ROPE TOO SHORT
North Carolina, Hanging Rock State Park, Moore's Wall

On November 5, a male climber (28) with limited experience and unfamiliarity with the Sentinel Buttress area of Moore's Wall rappelled to the end of his rope after missing the second rappel station. He noticed that he was short on rope approximately 75 feet from the base of the cliff. He did, however, have a belay rope attached, but it was too short as well.

Park personnel received call for assistance via a cell phone by a friend of the climber at the base of the cliff. The climber was instructed to reach behind himself to pull the last five feet of rope in front of him and to tie himself off while the rescue squad could get to his location and assess the situation. The climber was able to stand on a small ledge during the incident.

Rescuers lowered a rope; he clipped in, and was lowered to the base of the cliff. It took approximately three and a half hours to complete the rescue.
Analysis
All climbers should be prepared and able to initiate a self-rescue in situations like this. Familiarization with the climbing area is also a practical way to prevent incidents like this from occurring. (Source: Sam Koch – Hanging Rock State Park, and Aram Attarian)

FALL ON ROCK – NO KNOT ON END OF ROPE
North Carolina, Rumbling Bald

On December 18, my climbing partner, Adam (33), and I (34) were climbing Walk This Way (5.11b) located in the Hanging Chain area of Rumbling Bald. Neither of us had done this climb before. Our plan was for Adam to lead the route, lower, pull the rope, and then I would lead the route and clean it as I lowered. We had a copy of the older version of Lambert & Shull's Selected Climbs in North Carolina in which the route was labeled as 100 feet, and therefore, we believed our 70-meter rope (230 feet) to be adequate to lower on.

I belayed Adam with a Grigri. While lowering, about ten to 15 feet above the base of the climb, the end of the rope fed through the Grigri and Adam began to free fall. The base of the climb was a 70-degree boulder-strewn slope. He travelled a total of 30-40 feet, may have turned and glanced off an oven-sized rock or two before coming to rest in a relatively soft area of leaves and dirt. His injuries were primarily abrasions, bruises, and a deep laceration on his thumb. After assessment and some first aid, he was able to walk out and drive home. Later, reading the newest version of Selected Climbs... I found the route labeled as 150 feet (a critical change).

Analysis

I learned to climb and use equipment from friends and climbing partners and knew the importance of tying a knot in the end of the rope to close the system. Adam and I got into the habit of climbing single pitch routes with an adequate rope length and no knot tied at the end of the rope. No matter the circumstance, a closed system should always be employed. Reviewing the latest version of the guidebook, and not putting undue trust in any guidebook, is also an important lesson learned. (Source: Daryl MacInnes)

FALL ON ROCK, INADEQUATE PROTECTION, NO HARD HAT
Oregon, Rocky Butte

On May 14, while leading a fifth class route, Christian Steiner (27) fell approximately 50 feet, sustaining a fatal head injury. It is believed that he climbed well above his last protection placement before he lost his grip and fell. (Source: Jeff Scheetz, Portland Mountain Rescue)

FALL ON SNOW – FALLING ICE SHEET KNOCKED CLIMBER OFF, CLIMBING UNROPED
Oregon, Mount Hood, Southside

On June 9, Meredith Jacques (30) was ascending the Southside Route with 11 others. They were at the 10,000-foot level near the summit rocks when a "sliding sheet of ice" knocked her from her stance, resulting in a fall of about 300 feet. She sustained head, neck, and back injuries, but was in fair condition.

Analysis

Falling ice near the summit on Mount Hood is a frequent objective hazard whose risk can be minimized by timing. Earlier hours usually offer colder temperatures, which add some diurnal stability to hanging ice. (Source: Jeff Scheetz, Portland Mountain Rescue)

FALL ON ROCK – RAPPEL ERROR
Oregon, Beacon Rock State Park

On July 24, Nathan Turner (30) was on the second rappel of Jill's Thrill at Beacon Rock. But he had threaded the single rope through a fixed anchor with both ends of the rope over the ledge. This left the rope ends not visible. He then mistakenly centered the rope on the manufacturer's warning marking – six meters from the end. The uneven rope went un-noticed, as part of it was hung up out of view on a lower ledge. Without stopper knots and no belay backup device, Turner rappelled about 15 feet before his belay device passed the short end of the rope resulting in a 100-foot fatal free fall. (Source: Jeff Scheetz,

Portland Mountain Rescue)

(Editor's Note: Too many examples of this kind of error, which is why we have included the instructional section on rappelling this year.)

FALL ON ROCK – HIKING TURNS INTO CLIMBING TERRAIN, INEXPERIENCE
Oregon, North Sister

On September 24, Brian C. Jones (37) slipped on the 35-degree friable volcanic rock slope below the summit of North Sister and tumbled down about 1,000 vertical feet to his death.

Jones "…was scrambling on some of the terrain near his climbing partner and he slipped, started sliding, and then cart wheeled down the mountain," according to the report from Lane County Sheriff's volunteer SAR unit.

Analysis

North Sister is a fourth-class route under normal conditions, approached along the top of the south ridge by a faint "climber's way" high up along the west side of a gendarme called The Camel's Hump. The route then winds to the east side of a second gendarme, then traverses across an exposed, friable 35 degree slope called the "Terrible Traverse" just under the Prouty Pinnacles to a gully called "The Bowling Alley" that leads to the summit blocks. Many groups equipped with helmets and rock climbing skills will elect to set a hand line across this traverse and then belay (and rappel) the loose and often ice covered gully to the summit. Other gifted, trained, and experienced individuals have virtually run to the summit talus blocks.

End of summer thunderstorms had coated the steep volcanic scree slopes with snow and ice. Slips under these conditions can lead to uncontrollable falls. (Source: Robert Speik)

FALL ON ROCK, PROTECTION PULLED OUT, INADEQUATE CLOTHING AND EQUIPMENT
Oregon, Marsupial Crags

On November 14, Aaron Seemen (32) was climbing a 5.7, -mixed multi-pitch climb with a frequent rock climbing partner, Natalie Paden. He was leading pitch-4 of a five5-pitch route called "Birds in a Rut" on The Wombat formation among the Marsupial Crags. He led up off a big belay ledge, placed a cam, and then a stopper. Then he down-climbed back to a stance to take off his gloves that he had been climbing with because it was cold. As he climbed back up, he cleaned the cam. When he climbed past the Black Diamond stopper, it fell out when the direction of pull from the rope changed. He slipped and without an upper anchor, the belay was not functioning, so he fell 25 feet.

Not realizing how seriously he was injured, he painfully rappelled 20 feet to the larger ledge below. At this point, it was clear to them that they could not self-rescue. The climbers had left their cell phones and day packs with their rope bags at the foot of the climb, 200 feet below.

Luck alone enabled them to signal two fully equipped climbers who happened to be walking on the Burma Road over 1,200 feet below them. The two climbers, by luck again, a Paramedic and a Wilderness First Responder, called 911 from one of their own cell phones and then climbed up to the ledge, bringing gear, clothing, and shelter from the very cold winds during that long afternoon. It should be noted that Aaron and Natalie are also trained WFRs.

Several groups responded. He recalled that six men rigged the high angle anchors and lowered the rescue litter and that six to eight people assisted in carrying the belayed rescue litter down the long 45-degree scree slope. Reportedly, nineteen SAR volunteers were involved, and everything went well during a safe evacuation.

Analysis

Aaron rates himself as having a moderate level of experience and is able to lead climbs rated to 5.9. He noted that he should have placed protection at or above his stance when the stopper below him was dislodged by the climbing rope.

All of their extra clothing and other essential gear, including two cell phones, were on the scree slope below the rock climb. Had they been unable to get help from chance passers-by, Natalie would have had to rappel to the scree, and Aaron surely would have suffered the onset of hypothermia on that very cold and windy day. (Source: Robert Speik – based on interviews with the participants, witnesses, personal climbing knowledge of the venue, and on the Mission Report released by the Deschutes County Sheriff's Search and Rescue Unit)

FALL ON ROCK, NUT/CAM PULLED OUT, EXCEEDING ABILITIES
Tennessee, Sunset Rock, Chickamauga and Chattanooga National Military Park

The park received a report of a serious fall and injury to a male climber (23) beneath Sunset Rock in the park's Lookout Mountain area on the evening of July 27th. A pair of climbers started Friday the 13th (5.8+). This was their fifth and hardest route of the day, according to the partner. The climb itself is short and protects well with wires and cams. There's nothing tricky about the gear to an experienced climber, but the crux is strenuous—especially for climbers attempting an on-sight lead at their technical limit—and occurs at a bulge about 25 feet up. This is where the leader encountered difficulties. According to the partner, the leader had placed four pieces of protection when he started to "shake" and lose composure. He attempted to down-climb, but fell in the process, ripping his two highest pieces (a Trango cam and a medium sized BD stopper), and hit the ground. Both of these pieces were seen still attached to the rope lying on the ground.

Responding park and local rescuers treated his injuries and began a carryout up and to the rim of Sunset Rock. He was airlifted that evening to Erlanger Hospital in Chattanooga with a dislocated shoulder and a shattered left foot.

Analysis

Experienced climbers in the area reported that the pair were sport climbers and were new to traditional climbing with little/no experience placing gear. The injured climber had been doing all the leading that day on new gear consisting of Trango cams and wires with a set of Camalots apparently "on order". Witnesses also noted that earlier in the day the leader (later the patient) was having considerable difficulty placing gear on a 5.7 route and had to jump off the opening moves several times.

Poor preparation, limited skill and understanding on how to place gear, and route selection may have been the contributing factors leading to this accident. (Source: John McCutcheon, Supervisory Park Ranger, and others)

FALL ON ROCK – POOR COMMUNICATION
Texas, Enchanted Rock State Natural Area

On Saturday, April 16, several groups of climbers were climbing at or in close vicinity of the Echo Canyon and Triple Cracks area. These included a group of six climbers from Austin, three climbers from Houston, a group of approximately 15 Boy Scouts guided by the Mountain Madness guide service, and another smaller group guided by the OWA guide service.

Arik Yaacob (age unknown) in the Austin group was about to climb Grass Crack (5.10a) on a top-rope. Grass Crack is approximately 70 feet in length. Before Arik started, his belayer and another climber below realized that Arik would be the last person in their group to do the climb. They asked him if he was okay with cleaning the anchors, which consisted of two bolts. He confirmed that he was. They asked him if he had equipment that he could use to attach himself while cleaning, and he confirmed that he did. He then proceeded to climb and reached the anchors.

At the anchors, he attached himself to the bolts and called, "Off belay." The belayer verbally confirmed that he was taking Arik off belay, then disconnected his belay device and walked away. There is a mild positive slope at the top of this climb, which means the top is not visible from the bottom.

At the top, Arik rigged himself for lowering and yelled, "Take." He did not receive a verbal response. He yelled, "Take!" again. This time, he thought he felt the rope tighten and felt like he was being supported by it, so he assumed he was back on belay. However, climbers on the ground had not heard him yelling, "Take!" and so had not put him back on belay.

He disconnected himself from the anchors, called, "Lower me!" He leaned back and fell, hitting one boulder, then another, and then a tree. The base of the climb has many sharp rocks and uneven terrain; luckily, he landed in a very small flat area between the rocks. He slammed into the ground, landing on his back. Initially he did not move. He had fallen approximately 70 feet, from the anchors to the ground.

Initially, Arik did not appear to be breathing. His belayer, who had rushed to his side, was about to attempt CPR, but Arik suddenly started gasping for air and moaning. The OWA guide came over a few seconds later and stated he had Wilderness First Responder training. The OWA guide, along with a first-year medical student in the Houston group, and a guide from the Mountain Madness group, performed the initial assessment. Meanwhile, the head guide from the Mountain Madness group was able to scramble to a higher area with better cell phone reception and was able to contact the ranger station to request emergency response and a helicopter.

Approximately 20 minutes later, the EMTs arrived on foot. A helicopter arrived shortly after that and transported Arik to a hospital in Austin where he was diagnosed with six fractured ribs and multiple cuts and bruises. He is expected to make a full recovery.

Analysis

The primary mistake was made when Arik weighted the rope expecting to be on belay but had not received a verbal confirmation. This lack of communication was facilitated by the fact that there is no clear line of sight between the top anchors and the belayer. The large number of people in the area may have also been a factor, as witnesses said that the Boy Scouts and other climbers were being very loud. This could have made verbal communication even more difficult. Climbers and belayers are encouraged to use names when communicating with each other, especially in congested areas.

Following the fall, other climbers found his ATC and several quickdraws scattered around the area, including one hanging in the tree he hit. Later examination of his harness revealed a broken gear loop. A possible explanation for the damaged items is that the quickdraws were damaged on impact with one of the boulders and somehow snagged some protrusion, ripping the gear loop. Another possible explanation is that the gear loop caught some part of the tree and ripped. Either of these situations would explain the scattered gear and could have further contributed to slowing of the fall. Finally, the fact that he was pulling the rope through the anchors as he fell may also have been a small factor in slowing the fall.

Though there was no head injury, there could have been, and it should be noted that Arik was not wearing a helmet. (Source: Neil Higa – edited from his post on rockclimbing.com)

(Editor's Note: See Colorado, May 17 and July 9.)

SNAKEBITE
Virginia, Great Falls Park, Bird's Nest

JB (44) was bitten by a Copperhead snake on May 27 at the Bird's Nest area of Great Falls Park. I (Luciano Lima) was climbing at Bird's Nest in a group separate from the bitten climber. I had just scrambled to the top of the cliff to break down my anchor when I heard a yell from below. The climber had placed his hand on a ledge above his head (where he couldn't see) for balance and was bitten by a copperhead in the finger. He finished scrambling to the top where I along with another climber did our best to keep him calm and offered to accompany him to the ranger station. We knew it wasn't a "dry" bite because the climber's finger immediately began to swell.

The three of us walked back to the climber's lot and in the process called 911. I drove him to the park entrance and upon our arrival an ambulance and a fire truck were there to meet us.

Analysis

Keep your eyes open for snakes and avoid placing hands onto ledges beyond your line of sight. (Source: Luciano Lima)

(Editor's Note: As the climber didn't fall, this is not a climbing accident, but is included because each year there are a number of incidents involving critters interacting with climbers – including snakes, bees, and birds of prey.)

FALL ON ROCK, POOR COMMUNICATION
Virginia, Shenandoah National Park, Old Rag Mountain

Late on Sunday afternoon June 5, Old Rag Mountain Stewards staff was getting ready to start scenario training when a call came into the park that Dave Rockwell (50+) had taken a fifty-foot fall on the Skyline (aka PATC) Wall.

Initial descriptions of events leading to the injury were that someone in Dave's party led Dobie Gillis (5.8) a climb about halfway up the wall and set anchors for a top rope belay and then lowered to the ground. Based on initial reports, Dave tied into the end of the original lead rope and climbed to the mid-wall anchors. Upon reaching the anchors, Dave and his belayer somehow got their signals mixed up. The belayer thought Dave was off belay while Dave thought he was on still on belay. Thinking he was securely belayed, Dave intentionally placed all his weight on the un-secured belay line and fell fifty feet to the rocky ground where he sustained fractures to this left ankle, pelvis, and elbow. He was evacuated by NPS helicopter.

Analysis

The belay contract is a basic skill in climbing that many climbers take for granted.

It was very fortunate for Dave that ORMS had trained responders on the mountain and that the weather conditions were such that they were not stressing the patient. Most importantly the weather and time of day meant that a National Park helicopter could respond and rapidly evacuate him. (Source: Edited from a post on oldragpatrolsbyrsl-blook.blogspot.com/) *(Editor's Note: One of several this year.)*

FALL ON ROCK, ANCHOR FAILURE – UNFINISHED KNOT
Virginia, Blue Ridge Parkway, Ravens Roost,

During the mid-afternoon on June 15, Jonathan Sullivan (20) fell approximately 100 feet to his death at Ravens Roost Overlook along the Blue Ridge Parkway.

He and two partners had been top-rope climbing since 11:30 a.m. The group was top-roping. Sullivan made it about 100 feet when he paused to rest before the fall. Each had taken falls throughout the day and the top-rope system had functioned properly.

Analysis

According to reports, it was Sullivan's first day climbing outdoors. Investigators said the probable cause of the fall was the failure of a knot securing the one-inch tubular webbing anchor sling. The single sling anchor (non-redundant) extended from a large tree to the cliff edge. Evidence suggested that the person constructing the top rope anchor placed a "temporary" knot or hitch in the webbing to hold it in place but became distracted and never finished tying the knot to complete the anchor. Amazingly, others climbed and were lowered on the route without incident throughout the day. This incident illustrates the importance of a redundant anchor system and the need to check the anchor prior to climbing. (Source: Tony Gonzalez – on www2.wsls.com/news and Kurt Speers – Blue Ridge Parkway)

FALL INTO CREVASSE, CLIMBING UNROPED, UNFAMILIAR WITH ROUTE, PARTY SEPARATED, INEXPERIENCE
Washington, Mount Rainier, Fuerer Finger

On the morning of May 10, Tucker Taffe (34), Adam Fabrikant (24), Bill Haas (24), and Nate Goodman (23) left their camp on the Wilson Glacier at approximately 02:45 to climb the Fuhrer Finger Route of Mount Rainier. About 0830, while ascending the route using skins and skis, unroped, and at 13,200 feet, Tucker Taffe fell into a crevasse and dropped approximately 75 feet. Immediately after the fall, the party established anchors and tried to communicate with their fallen partner. They did not, however, try to execute a self-rescue or access Taffe.

One climber left the scene to get help, and traversed, alone and unprotected, across the top of the Nisqually Icefall and down the Ingraham Direct route. Meanwhile, the remaining two members continued trying to establish communication, but again, did not attempt to reach the fallen climber.

At 0955, a team of 12 Alpine Ascents International guides encountered the reporting party near Ingraham Flats. The AAI team notified the NPS with the information they had just received. The guides and the Incident Commander agreed (as per a pre-existing contractual component that requires guide services operating in the park to respond/assist with incidents) that due to their proximity, it would be of great benefit for the party of guides to climb to the location of the fallen climber and provide what assistance they could.

Attempts to acquire a suitable helicopter from civilian vendors around the state proved a great challenge, because certified pilot/ship combinations were scarce on this morning. A Bell-210 type-2 helicopter from Worldwind Helicopters was eventually ordered, as it was available with an ETA of less than one hour.

At 1055, a ground team of four climbing rangers was dispatched from Paradise to Camp Muir as a contingency team should aviation operations not be feasible.

At 1103 the guides reached the location of the crevasse into which Taffe had fallen. At 1130, a guide descended into the crevasse and at 1211 reported hearing "moaning". However the fallen climber could not be seen, as he was buried under about 1.5 meters of snow. Another guide (a paramedic) descended to assist and the two guides used an avalanche beacon to determine the Taffe's precise location under the snow and began to excavate the snow to uncover him. At 1220 they exposed Taffe's head but found him unresponsive and "exhibiting agonal breathing" (gasping, labored breathing, accompanied by strange vocalizations). They cleared the snow from in front of his head and almost immediately after, Taffe ceased breathing and became pulseless. Despite the fact that they were working within the tight confines of the crevasse and that much of Taffe's body was still buried under snow, the two guides attempted to get him breathing again. At 1248 the guides reported that Taffe still wasn't breathing and was wedged tightly into the crevasse.

The two guides climbed out of the crevasse and after another attempt to haul the body from the surface, the guide team was directed by the NPS at 1418 to cease their efforts as it seemed apparent that alternate extrication means would be necessary.

Following extrication by four rangers, the deceased was flown to Kautz Heli-base at 1645 and released to the Pierce County Coroner later that night.

Analysis

While the decision to go unroped may appear foolhardy, the decision was not altogether without reason, as the terrain below the fall site dictated the party's initial decision to travel unroped. There is about 1000 feet of climbing below the site of the incident, which is steep, uncrevassed terrain in a couloir, and many parties choose to travel this section un-roped. Above the couloir, many climbers follow a steep, broken ridgeline; however, a lack of familiarity with the route led to this party to traverse towards the top of the Nisqually Cleaver, which is a large, obvious terrain feature toward which the party may have gravitated. The traverse, as well as the terrain above it, is heavily crevassed. Interviews with the surviving members of the party revealed that the party failed to recognize the imminent crevasse hazard, as the party did not re-rope and continued to ascend. This decision may have been compounded by the fact that the party had separated, somewhat due to differences in fitness and speed of travel (they were utilizing different climbing techniques - Taffe had skis/ skins on, while the others had not yet put their approach skis back on). Note that while Taffe was using skis as an approach tool, he was not, by definition, "skiing" when the incident occurred.

The party's relative inexperience and lack of training (to respond to a crevasse fall) left them unable to descend to their partner - despite the fact that they had the appropriate equipment to do so. While Taffe had fallen approximately 75 feet, he had suffered no significant trauma (per the coroner's report). However, he had been buried under approximately 1.5 meters of snow and ice from the collapsed "roof" of the crevasse. Unable to extract/unbury himself or clear the snow in front of his face, Taffe spent approximately four hours buried under the snow.

Being prepared for a crevasse fall includes not only carrying the proper equipment, but also having the practiced skills to execute a self-rescue. Unfortunately, many aspiring climbers don't take the opportunity to train themselves in real-life conditions (overhanging edges, etc.) and find they need to seek outside help. In this incident, qualified help was "only" four hours away. In most circumstances, even in a National Park, where rescue services are more readily available, it will take hours for responders to arrive due to the logistics associated with access, helicopter availability, personnel numbers, etc. In a situation where minutes count, it is imperative that climbers be able to execute a self-rescue. Even if substantial injuries exist, being able to provide patient care (such as maintaining a patient's airway, providing warmth, etc.) is critical to a patient's wellbeing in the hours to follow. Clearly, doing so may pose some risk to the self-rescuers, especially if they are operating beyond their experience level. In this case, rescuing their fallen partner may have posed significant risk due to their inexperience, much as the climber who descended alone to seek help through heavily crevassed, unfamiliar terrain, exposed himself to significant risk. Self-rescue requires having a practiced action plan, good communication, and foresight to avoid an "incident within an incident". (Source: Brian Hasebe – Park Ranger, The News Tribune, Tacoma, WA, and Mount Rainier News Releases)

EXHAUSTION – POSSIBLE AMS OR HACE, FALL ON ICE/SNOW, WEATHER
Washington, Mount Rainier, Liberty Ridge

On June 12, Rob Plankers (50), Brad Clement (40), and Tanya Clement (48) departed White River for a summit attempt via the Liberty Ridge route. They were experienced climbers and were well equipped. On the last day of their ascent, Rob Plankers became exhausted, moderately hypothermic, and possibly frostbitten. Their slow ascent forced them to bivouac at 13,900 feet on a wide, windswept shoulder above the route, where they were exposed to high winds and drifting snow overnight. The following morning, Planker's partners were unable to get him walking from their camp and were forced to leave him to seek assistance. They left him attached to a two-point mountaineering anchor with his sleeping bag, bivy sack, stove, and fuel. They contacted a ranger on Emmons Glacier at 5:00 p.m. that evening. Two teams of climbing rangers headed to his location, one team from Camp Schurman and the other from Camp Muir. One of the teams was forced to turn back at 12,100 feet due to high winds at 1:00 a.m. Members of the second team spent the night in a snow cave and resumed their efforts to reach the climber at 5:00 a.m. the next morning. A rescue team was inserted by Chinook helicopter (214th Airborne – Joint Base Ft. Lewis-McChord) and found some of Planker's gear at the point where his partners left him, but were unable to find Planker. Air search revealed a 2,000-foot-long track leading down a 50-degree ice and snow-covered slope. The track indicated intermittent airborne periods and ended at an icefall below Liberty Wall. No signs of Planker were found during a thorough visual search of the slide area. Additional air resources were called in to assist, but the search was called off at 4:00 p.m. due to high winds. Limited visual searching by both ground and air teams continued throughout the season in case melting snow revealed additional clues.

Analysis

Rob Planker had summited Mount Rainier five times prior to this attempt, so he had appropriate expectations for the length and difficulty of the climb. His current fitness, however, was reportedly a precipitating factor, as it led to a forced bivy high on the exposed shoulder of Liberty Cap. The party's decision to bivy high on the route instead of "pushing through" resulted in additional exposure to the high winds and low temps, and may have also increased the likelihood of AMS or HACE further debilitating the climber.

The decision to leave Rob Planker alone while the Clements went for help may, at first glance, seem callous, but was likely the most appropriate decision for the team. The Clements (a married couple) were unfamiliar with the route and would have been climbing solo through glaciated terrain had they split up.

It's possible that Planker tried to stand up, and in the process, yanked his anchor upwards and out prior to falling, as the anchor material was not found on scene by searchers.

The party's decision to not take a communication device, while admirable in some sense, may have also increased the time required to get help. As it was, the NPS was already poised to initiate a search, which sped up the overall response, but sadly, to no avail. The lesson here is to bring a communication device – and to use it appropriately. (Source: Brian Hasebe - Park Ranger, The News Tribune, Tacoma, WA, and Mount Rainier News Releases)

LOSS OF CONTROL ON GLISSADE - FALL INTO CREVASSE/MOAT, POOR VISIBILITY, MISPERCEPTION, NO HARD HAT
Washington, Mount Baker

On July 2, my girlfriend Sheryl Costello (34) and I (45) climbed the Coleman Headwall route on Mount Baker in excellent conditions. That afternoon we descended the normal route to a camp on an outcrop near the bottom of the glacier.

Conditions deteriorated that evening, with high winds, sleet, and moderate intermittent rain showers. The winds decreased by morning but the rain and fog continued. The entire approach route was still covered with several meters of snow at this date.

We encountered several men from a Canadian party near a feature known as the "hogback" which is about 1600 meters, just below the glaciated terrain. A descending party has the option of walking down the hogback or glissading the adjacent snowfield. The area's standard climbing map indicates a "dangerous moat" about halfway down the snowfield. Our climb the previous day indicated that most such features were still covered by solid snow bridges. We decided as a group that a glissade would not pose an unusual risk.

Visibility remained poor (less than 20 meters at times) when we began the glissade about 11:30 a.m. Sheryl went first and immediately disappeared into the fog. Two or three of the Canadian party and I followed her. Partway down the snowfield the figures of the Canadians materialized out of the mist. They were investigating a small gap (about one by three meters) in the snow, which had considerable water flowing through it. A glissade path was visible below the gap, continuing into the forest.

We bypassed the gap and presumed that the glissade path indicated that Sheryl had continued down the snowfield. At the bottom, another 200 vertical meters below the gap, we gathered again. Sheryl was not in the group. The glissade trail continued down into the forest and we presumed that she had continued lower. As a precaution, I returned upslope to the gap in the snow. After shouting into the hole (no response) and examining the hole for scrapes, breakage, or other signs of entry (inexplicably, there were none), I returned to the bottom of the snowfield, and we began a search of the immediate area.

I suggested the possibility of descending into the hole in the seemingly unlikely event that Sheryl had fallen in without leaving any indication. However, I was counseled – wisely, it turned out – by a member of the Canadian party with search and rescue experience that, lacking any such indication, such an attempt was a risk.

As a group, we searched the trail down to the Heliotrope Ridge trailhead and asked ascending climbers whether they had seen Sheryl. All of them answered in the negative. Upon arrival at the trailhead, we alerted emergency response. Local USFS personnel, Deputy Mark Jilk of Whatcom County Sheriff, and Bellingham Mountain Rescue responded in about two hours; meanwhile, a Border Patrol helicopter conducted a brief aerial search.

I accompanied BMR personnel, who brought equipment to the snowfield and rigged a lowering line at the hole by about 4:00 p.m. An initial search to a depth of about eight meters revealed a number of lost items (gloves, snowshoes, etc.), none of which were Sheryl's. BMR continued the search effort in the woods and terrain nearby, pending arrival of a dry suit that would permit a deeper descent into the hole.

The dry suit arrived after sunset and the lowering line was re-rigged. One of the BMR people, equipped with a high-intensity light and a radio, was lowered into the hole between 10:00 and 11:00 p.m. Sheryl's body and a number of items of her equipment were identified about 15-20 meters down. There was no chance that she had survived the fall and subsequent immersion. BMR determined that a recovery would not be an acceptable risk. Her body and much of her equipment were recovered about six weeks later when conditions under the snow had sufficiently stabilized.

Analysis

Poor visibility was a significant factor. The fog and the convex slope likely prevented her from seeing the hole until it was too late to arrest. Nobody saw Sheryl disappear into the hole.

The snow in and around the hole was unchanged. I still don't know how a climber wearing a pack could fall into a relatively small hole like that and leave no scrape marks on the sides of the hole or cause no breakage of the snow around the opening.

Neither one of us were wearing helmets. We believed (incorrectly, obviously) that since we were below the glaciated terrain, we were past the dangers of the approach route. The autopsy indicated she suffered a fractured skull in the fall.

It's possible, though unknown, that the hole had been covered with a snow bridge until the previous night's rainfall.

The accident site is a "known" hazard among local climbers, and was adequately identified on the map. However, due to the poor visibility, we did not know where we were in relation to the hazard.

I wish to commend Deputy Jilk and BMR for their bravery, professionalism, and compassion in attempting to rescue my girlfriend. Sheryl was an experienced alpinist with ascents of a number of glaciated volcanoes on two continents to her credit. Her loss is a terrible tragedy for me, her family, and everyone who knew her. (Source: John Korfmacher)

(Editor's Note: We thank John for his willingness to write this difficult piece. In many ways, it is uncannily similar to the incident that follows.)

LOSS OF CONTROL ON GLISSADE - FALL INTO CREVASSE/MOAT, INEXPERIENCE
Washington, North Cascades, Aasgard Pass

On July 3 about 10:30 a.m., Julia Rutherford (21) was glissading down the Colchuck Lake side of Aasgard Pass with three other people: her boyfriend Peter Borschowa, his father, and a friend. She fell into a moat, down a high-volume sub-snow-surface waterfall and was swept downstream under the snow.

Peter Borschowa said he heard a scream and then helplessly watched as Julia Rutherford disappeared into a crevasse. He searched at the base of the waterfall but he could not see the victim and she did not respond when he called her name. It appeared she was unreachable without a rope. He then ran out to the Stuart Lake Trailhead for help. Three other witnesses went in separate directions for help, finding two more parties at the top of the pass, one from the Seattle Mountaineers with ropes and one from the Washington Alpine Club.

While two people stayed at the top of Aasgard Pass and called 911 at 11:00 a.m., the remaining first responders descended to the accident scene, which was approximately one third of the way up the pass. The slope was steep enough to be a black diamond or double black diamond at a ski area and we observed a glissade path leading directly over the waterfall. We shouted Julia's name into the base of the waterfall but received no response.

The remaining two members of the party were distraught and had begun descending very slowly. One had a shoulder injury from an out-of-control glissade that had preceded the primary accident. One first responder descended the pass with these additional victims and monitored their condition.

At the accident scene, we dug a hole five feet from the waterfall, built a snow anchor, and lowered a volunteer from our group into the waterfall to search for the victim. She was able to retrieve Rutherford's ice axe about 15 feet down the waterfall, but was not able to see Rutherford through just a 1½ foot aperture through which the water was flowing at the bottom of the space.

We then sent a small group up the pass to contact 911 again while another group started marking the slope for any helicopter rescue. We also marked the glissade path with sticks well above the waterfall to warn others of the danger ahead. There was only one shovel in our group and we used it throughout the day to dig more holes, although the snow got progressively deeper away from the waterfall. As a precaution, we were on belay while shoveling.

About 2:00 p.m., an off-duty rescuer from Seattle Mountain Rescue, who had familiarity with the terrain, arrived and instructed us to dig a hole in a particular spot. While we were digging, a helicopter from Whidbey Naval Air Station inserted two corpsmen. One of them belayed off three snow anchors and lowered into the twelve-foot deep hole when it reached the watercourse. He located Rutherford's body approximately 45 feet from the waterfall. The first responders extricated the corpsman and the victim out, approximately 6 hours and 45 minutes after she had fallen in.

Analysis

It struck many of the first responders how relatively safe and normal the path must have looked from above. All that was visible was a lip beyond which the path was not visible for a few feet.

But there are several lessons and reminders here. First, don't glissade if you can't see the run-out and keep speed under control at all times. Second, be very cautious of moats and other sub-surface hazards in late spring and consider plunge stepping, being roped up, and carrying a beacon, probe and shovel.

The rescue came with its own lessons. First is just the sheer length of time that it takes to get trained rescuers on the scene. Next, Peter Borschowa spread the word far and wide on his descent to the trailhead, which was important in getting the manpower and skills necessary for the rescue. Third, personal radios would have been very helpful because we only had cellphone service at the top of the pass – and that was a 30 to 45 minute climb away. (Source: Will Kruse – Washington Alpine Club, Eileen Kutscha and Erica Cline – Seattle Mountaineers, and www.komonemews.com)

ILLNESS AND FROSTBITE (TWO INCIDENTS)
Washington, Mount Rainier

While on a summit climb on the morning of July 13 about 9:00 a.m., Dr. Walter Leonard (56) experienced extreme pain in his right abdomen and back. The climbers accompanying him called the NPS Ranger Nick Hall, who was on duty at Camp Muir, and explained that their patient was non-ambulatory and in extreme pain. Ranger Hall called Climbing Ranger Supervisor, Brian Hasebe, who became Incident Commander. The 214th General Support Aviation Brigade at joint base Ft. Lewis-McChord was called and accepted the mission to retrieve Dr. Leonard.

Meanwhile another incident unfolded within the same party. Sergeant Derek Ford (23) who was at 10,800 feet on the Disappointment Cleaver, began suffering from frostbite at the end of a leg that had been amputated. So these two injuries were communicated to the US Army Reserve unit at Ft. Lewis-McChord. The NPS and USAR formulated a plan to extricate both injured parties. Because of a cloud deck around Mount Rainier, rangers drove to Ft. Lewis where they briefed and boarded the US Army Reserve CH-47 Chinook helicopter. Rangers Philippe Wheelock, Chris Kalman, and Jonathon Bowman flew from Ft. Lewis to the summit and picked up one patient. Then they flew to 10,800 feet and used the hoist and jungle penetrator to extricate the second patient. The patients and rangers were transported back to Madigan Army Medical Center.

As an aside note, many of the guide services were involved in this operation due to the fact that this was the Camp Patriot summit climb which is a benefit climb for disabled veterans. Many of the guide services had been donating their own employees or resources in a volunteer capacity. Some of the party leaders were former guide service employees. The guides were the initial reporting parties and with the patients until the rangers took over during the extrication process. (Source: Brian Hasebe - Park Ranger and Mount Rainier News Releases)

(Editor's Note: this is a good illustration of how the park's rangers and support services such as Fort Lewis-McChord work together to provide help for climbers – and hikers – in need.)

FALL ON SNOW – LOSS OF CONTROL ON VOLUNTARY GLISSADE, INADEQUATE CLOTHING AND EQUIPMENT
Washington, Mount Rainier, Near Camp Muir

On the afternoon of July 17, a group of friends from Fort Lewis Air Force Base were coming down from Camp Muir after a training climb for a later summit attempt. Visibility was poor that day, and at some point the party got sidetracked and began to descend off the actual climbers' path. They began to glissade; however, Mike Pickerel (40) broke away from the group and began to go down a blind hill. Unable to see where he was going, Pickerel slid approximately 12 feet down a steep slope on the backside of McClure Rocks and ended his uncontrolled glissade when he hit a rock outcropping. Pickerel reported he had broken his ankle and dislocated his shoulder, so two members of the party walked back down to Paradise to notify rangers.

One of the climbing rangers was able to ski down from Camp Muir and was first on scene to begin treatment. Four other rangers with a litter package hiked up from Paradise to the patient's location and began to package the patient. At nightfall the entire group of rangers, climbers, and the patient began their descent via the lower skyline/golden gate trail, sliding the patient on a cascade sled. Steep slopes called for several high angle lowers before the litter was on fairly flat terrain. Pickerel was placed in an ambulance and taken to Madigan hospital.

Analysis

Once the accident had occurred, the party was hasty to designate three members to hike down to Paradise to request help. They had some food and water; however, most of them were not prepared to stay out overnight and that is why only a few were able to assist in the carryout. When Glen Kessler arrived on the scene, he had to use his own gear and clothing to keep the patient warm. Nobody in the party had a rope or any other gear necessary to assist in the carryout. Although the party was treating their hike as a training mission for a further summit date, they had brought minimal supplies with them to camp Muir. Also, even though visibility was low, the party was disoriented in relation to where they thought they had initially hunkered down once their friend had been injured. The party did have a GPS, which was being used to help locate their location prior to Kessler's discovery of the party. As a general rule, it is not safe to glissade down a path where the runout is not visible. (Source; Sam Cowan, Park Ranger)

FALL ON ROCK – RAPPEL ERROR, FATIGUE, POSSIBLE HASTE
Washington, Beacon Rocks State Park

On July 24, Nathan Turner (30) and his partner were in the second rappel of "Jill's Thrill," a common descent route for the area. The first rappel placed the two climbers onto a small ledge without incident. They lowered safely onto the ledge and setup their second rappel by threading the rope through the second set of chain anchors. Setup took longer than expected. Turner mentioned to his partner that it felt like he'd been "pulling rope a long time." After this was said, they saw black markings on the rope signaling what they believed was the middle of their rope. Turner threw the side of the rope he'd been pulling up over the ledge and then setup his ATC to rappel. Last checks were made and he began his descent.

It started well enough. No failure occurred when the climber first took himself off his personal anchor. The failure occurred after a few seconds of lowering. Turner's partner heard a loud "snap!" and then watched the rope rapidly unravel through the chains. He and two witnesses climbing an adjacent route then watched Turner free-fall, strike "Snag Ledge" below, and disappear from sight ultimately falling to the floor.

Analysis

It is believed that the rope wasn't set with half the rope equally on each side of the anchor chains. What likely occurred is that when they initially missed the halfway markings, Turner kept pulling and centered the rope on the end warning marks. The rope they used was a 70 meter (9.4mm diameter) Petzl Fuze, which has markings both at the middle of the rope and at six meters (~20ft) from the ends. The markings in the middle are a solid black line. The ones on the ends are dashed black lines. The rope itself was blackened over a season of use but was in excellent condition. The rope with these markings is no longer in production. The surviving partner made contact with the manufacturer–Petzl–a few months after the accident and he was told they had decided–actually prior to this accident–that they had weren't going to produce future ropes with any end markings on their ropes until the CE–European Committee for Standardization–established a unifying standard for all manufacturers to follow. The process for this standard is ongoing.

It is unsure exactly when he started his free fall. If he had been only rappelling on six meters of rope, the start of his fall would have been in-line with what they observed when he fell around 6-12 meters to his first contact point on Snag Ledge. This makes their account consistent enough to support the misbalanced rope hypothesis. The "snap" his partner heard at the start of the fall was likely the end of the rope whipping through the ATC. It's not clear how the two mistook the markings aside from attributing it to end of day fatigue.

Nathan Turner was experienced having mountaineered for seven-plus years and had done technical rock climbing for two years. His partner was in his 4th year of technical rock climbing. Rappelling was not new to them.

For this scenario to be plausible, how could such a misbalanced and fast-pulling rope not slip free if it was so misbalanced? The proposed answer is that it wasn't likely an issue of six meters of freestanding rope balancing 64 meters of freestanding rope. It was more likely six meters of rope balancing the distance from the anchor to Snag Ledge (~10m) where the thrown end of the rope had snagged (hence the name Snag Ledge). That unfortunate rope accumulation on the ledge left Turner in a situation where he wouldn't have noticed the weight imbalance unless he or others around him looked at the ends and noticed something wrong.

Only one rope-end was confirmed to have had a Figure-8 knot. The other side could not be confirmed to have had a knot. It is unclear why. The most likely explanation is the knot did not get re-tied when the rope was re-threaded through the next set of chains. There was an irregularity in procedure that could have been the cause of the misstep. Turner's partner recalls it was he, not Turner, who actually did the re-threading through the chains. After that there was an exchange like: "Hey, do you need to do anything with this?" "Nah, we're good." Turner's partner did not re-tie a knot. (He wasn't instructed to). If that rope was allowed to just freely lower and hadn't ever gone back to Turner to tie the standard Figure 8 knot, it would explain how the knot didn't get put back onto the rope. So, sometime when the two partners were shifting around to setup the rappel and fighting end-of-day fatigue, it's likely that tying a back-up Figure 8 just didn't happen and went unnoticed by both of them – as with the rope markings.

In prior documented cases of similar rappelling mistakes (of which two were found in prior publications of ANAM), common traits shared with this incident were:

- Using ropes with extra markings.
- Rappelling done at the end of the day.
- The full rappelling path view was obstructed
- Stopper knots weren't used (or verifiably used).
- The longer end of the rope stuck to something so the weight misbalance wasn't noticed.

(Source: Michael Aubrey, The Columbian, Portland, OR, and www.supertopo.com)

(Editor's Note: There were a few other "loss of control while glissading" and "altitude illness incidents" on Mount Rainier, but the examples provided in the narra-

tives here cover the ground.)

FALL ON ROCK – OVERCONFIDENCE ON FOURTH-CLASS TERRAIN
Washington, North Cascades, Washington Pass

The plan of the day (August 13) was to do a bunch of routes on the Early Winter Spires from 5.6 to 5.9. We were on the ascent/descent gully trail to the col between Liberty Bell and Concord tower in good time. Racking up, we raced up Becky's route as a warm up (5.6, three pitches) and rapped back to the col. Concord Tower was the next choice, but it was very busy with other parties, so we quickly packed up and headed back down the gully to find something less busy. The gully is 3rd and 4th class and VERY loose, so, we kept our helmets on. I remember the first time I came here I was very careful, but now having done it so much, I was just scooting along with no care in the world, using one hiking pole for balance. Around 12:30 p.m. about one third of the way down, my foot slipped as a loose rock moved. I lost my balance and came down hard on my right leg, which broke my right tibia and fibula in multiple places. I was in a steep section, so I pulled myself to a little better location. I had a SAM splint and tape, so I moved my leg back around to the correct position and tried to support it as best I could. At this point Todd (who I did not know) came down off his climb to see if I was ok. He had a SPOT device (we had no cell coverage). I had him activate it (I feel bad for Todd's folks who might have thought he was the victim). At 12:45 p.m. I had my partner Crystal hike back out to the car and drive until she came to a phone. She called 911 and advised that a helicopter would be required due to the nature of the injury and the location and terrain. She then stayed with the SAR people down at the road to provide additional advise.

The SAR reached me at 6:00 p.m. and fixed an additional splint. Then the US Navy helicopter from Whidby Island lowered Brent McIntyre on a long line to extract me and take me to Omak Hospital (7:30 p.m.) where I underwent an operation that included15 screws and two plates.

Analysis

Fine weather, the SPOT device, no wind, strong SAR and Navy support, having a SAM splint, basic medical supplies and training made this a fairly straightforward rescue.

Being an experienced climber made me over-confident on anything less that steep class-5 climbing. Just because you go up and down a gully a dozen times with no mishap doesn't mean you can relax and be complacent. Could this have been avoided? Absolutely! If the weather was poor, if I had been climbing alone as I often do, could it have been MUCH worse? Yes! I did not give the mountain environment the respect it deserved. (Source: Jason Wheeler – 40)

FALLING ROCK - TRIGGERED BY PARTY ABOVE, POOR POSITION
Washington, North Cascades, Forbidden Peak, West Ridge

About 6:30 pm. on August 18, Jay Kullyman (42) and his partner had completed the rappels of the gully (climber's) left of the standard couloir on the West Ridge of Forbidden Peak. They were standing on snow when they heard warnings of "Rock!" from above. Both tried to evade the rock-fall, but Kullyman sustained deep lacerations above one knee with resulting significant blood loss.

He was lowered and assisted to camp by his partner, the two climbers who had triggered the rock and another party of four. They reached camp after midnight. The group decided assistance was needed and a satellite phone call was placed to 911 by a commercial group, also camped at the upper bivy sites in Boston Basin.

Rangers for NCNP responded by both ground and helicopter. The injured climber was evacuated by helicopter the following morning.

Analysis

Forbidden Peak is one of the most appealing and sought mountaineering objectives in the North Cascades. Various outstanding routes exist on multiple ridges and faces. The West Ridge is arguably the easiest approach and most frequently completed route to the summit with various descent options.

Its popularity does draw many parties, especially on fair weather weekends, creating the standard hazard of rock-fall especially on descent of the gullies used to obtain and descend the ridge.

Observations of the obvious rock-fall in the gully showed that there was potential in this incident for more casualties. The higher party had tested a large rock for stability, sending it down the gully toward both climbers, as well as climbers below them. It is fortunate that only the one climber was hit.

Jay Kuyllman reported that he has been a trad and ice climber for 20-years And that his has partner even more experience. He said, "We are certainly not cutting edge guys, but have both done some of the classic lines in the Tetons, Wind Rivers, we have both done Rainier, Baker, and Stuart, as well as some of the classic climbs in the French Alps. 'The lesson' we already knew (was) the danger of being down first on an alpine route. We realized the party above us had less experience, but we had observed them several times on the route and they seemed careful." (Source: Kelly Bush, Wilderness District Ranger, North Cascades National Park, and Jay Kuyllman)

PULLED OFF A LOOSE BLOCK – FALL ON ROCK
Washington, Mount Stuart

I was climbing the West Ridge of Mount Stuart on September 7 when I pulled off a loose block and took a 60-foot fall. We were roped up, belaying the pitch. We had decent protection in, but it was a low 5th-class pitch and the gear spacing reflected that.

I'm still recovering from my injuries (concussion, four fractured ribs, collapsed lung, scapula, laceration on lower leg requiring surgery, etc.) but am at the point where I am able to write it all down.

We failed to bring a cell phone and did not have any other kind of device.

I hope some climber somewhere can learn from my incident and be just that much more safe.

I'm also a member of a local mountain rescue unit and a rescue tech on a heli-team. Overall, (this rescue) was a fantastically coordinated and successful rescue. (Source: Miles McDonough – 28)

FALL ON ROCK, NO HARD HAT
West Virginia, New River Gorge National River

On June 5th, a male climber (22) was leading Layback and Enjoy It (5.10) located at the Bubba City climbing area. The following is a synopsis of the most likely scenario that occurred causing the fall of approximately 10-12 feet.

As he was approaching the 4th or 5th bolt he yelled, "Falling!" He came off the rock and inverted, striking his head approximately ten to 12 feet below, knocking him unconscious. His belayer lowered him to the ground and 911was initiated. Health Net Air Medical Services flew him to Charleston Area Medical Center.
Analysis
The climber was not wearing a helmet at the time of the fall. (Source: Frank Sellers—District Ranger and Randy Fisher—Park Ranger New River Gorge National River)

FALL ON ROCK, PROTECTION PULLED OUT
West Virginia, New River Gorge National River

During the evening of June 13, a female (25) was climbing Biohazard (5.10a) a 65' trad route located on the Fern Creek Party Wall. She was almost at the top of the route when she fell about 15 feet and slammed into the wall, knocking herself unconscious. She had just placed a cam for protection and was leaning back to rest when the placement failed and she fell about 15 feet. The next piece of protection held and her belayer was able to hold the fall. Although wearing a helmet, the impact caused her to lose consciousness for about 30 seconds. After regaining consciousness, she was lowered to the base of the cliff and carried out to a waiting ambulance by Fayette County's high-angle rescue team, assisted by local firefighters. She was then flown to Charleston for evaluation.

Although she complained of dizziness, hearing loss and back pain, her injuries were not deemed severe and she was soon released. (Source: Jeff West—Chief Ranger, New River Gorge National River)

PROTECTION BOLT PULLED OUT
West Virginia, Meadow River

Late in the day on June 23, a bolt pulled out while a climber was lowering off a sport route. The climber struck the ground and broke his leg.

The accident took place at a crag along the Meadow River located in the New River Gorge area. This location is not in a guidebook, but is used by local guides and climbers. The male climber (25) and belayer were part of a large combined summer-camp group originating from two separate climbing gyms.

The specific route is an uncompleted tagged sport project of unknown difficulty. The climb, which is roughly 55 feet from ground to anchor, follows a steep slab for five bolts to a roughly horizontal roof that is approximately six to eight feet horizontal. There were two bolts in the roof with another at the lip. From the lip of the roof, the route continues up a short steep face to a two-bolt anchor. The two roof bolts, the bolt at the lip, and the two anchor bolts had draws in situ. The bolt that pulled out is a 2.5" by 3/8" stainless steel wedge anchor. It is assumed that all the other bolts on the route are of similar stock.

The group had been climbing for most of the day on 5.8 to 5.10 routes and the victim had already led several climbs. In the afternoon, the group was wrapping and cleaning routes to prepare to leave. The victim wanted to climb an additional route and selected this unknown climb. The Instructor questioned the victim on whether he was able to climb this route. The victim stated that he was capable of climbing the lower section and would lower off if he were unable to climb past the roof section.

Around 5:00 p.m., the victim led up five bolts with some aid to the roof section, where he clipped the first fixed draw. He attempted the moves and fell. His belayer caught him without incident. He hung on this bolt for approximately five minutes, before he decided to lower from it. As he lowered, he cleaned his draws.

At the second bolt from the ground, the victim un-weighted the rope and stepped onto a ledge to unclip the draw. As he re-weighted the rope to continue his lower, the lone bolt from which he was suspended pulled out. Save that one bolt, none of the bolts above him were clipped to the rope. This created about 50+ feet of slack in the system instantly and the victim fell eight to ten feet to the ground.

Upon landing, he fell backwards down the slope about eight feet into a bank of rhododendrons. His feet hit first and he did not hit his back or head. He was in an upright but reclined position when he landed. Bystanders called for help and the Instructor was able to assist.

The victim was in pain and had a deformed left ankle. Upon receiving a description of what had happened, the Instructor placed the victim in a hands on stable position and supported his head and back from movement. Approximately five to eight minutes passed before additional assistance arrived.

One of the instructors splinted the victim's left foot and ankle with a SAM splint and bandages. The group improvised a litter and carried him to the parking area, approximately 75 meters downhill. He was taken to Summersville Hospital where an x-ray revealed a fractured tibia.

Analysis

The victim engaged in a typical sport climbing practice of lowering from a single high point and collecting draws on the way down. The belayer made no errors while belaying. The injuries were a direct result from falling from about 8-10 feet above the ground.

When the high bolt pulled out, it placed too much slack in the system and the victim fell to the ground. It was not possible for the belayer to correct for this.

The bolt in question was placed directly in the roof and came away under an outward pull directly along the shaft. The bolt had only been in the rock about ten months. The bolt had a fixed draw on it, the lowest on the route to be so equipped. A visual inspection revealed damaged threads on the shaft that was in the rock. There were damaged threads on the shaft in several locations.

The nut on the bolt shaft was fixed and unable to spin. This is the location of the nut's fixed position on the shaft. It will not turn in either direction. The collar is not fully engaged. This is the condition in which the bolt was found on the ground.

There were also significant hammer marks on the shaft, nut and hanger. The question is whether excessive force was used to drive the bolt into the hole. The cause could have been poor hammering technique or the hole-diameter may have been too small, creating the need for more force to drive the bolt stud into the hole. The angle of the climb suggests it would have been awkward to strike a clean hammer blow, let alone several in a row.

The next day the Instructor and a local climber went back to the accident scene. The local climber rappelled the route to inspect the remaining bolts and remove the remaining hangers. Due to the angle of the climb and the one missing bolt, he was unable to reach the two highest bolts on the face below the roof. He was able to inspect the anchor and two bolts below it (including one in the roof), plus the first three bolts of the climb. Upon arriving at each bolt, all of them appeared and felt solid. None of the hangers were spinning and none of the nuts were loose.

Upon attempting to remove all of the hangers he could reach, however, the inspecting climber was only able to achieve, on average, one complete turn of his wrench, before the studs began to spin in their holes. One should not be able to rotate the shaft of a bolt in a hole simply by loosening the nut. One should be able unscrew the nut without turning the shaft of the bolt.

He was able to remove only the hanger from the climb's second bolt. The remaining nuts were fixed in place on their studs. The conditions of those remaining bolts confirm that the threads were damaged and their collars were never fully engaged. The two climbers left the stuck hangers in place, but wrapped with copious amounts of athletic tape around all of them.

The excessive marks on the bolt, hanger and nut, plus the threads not working may have been an indication that the bolt had too much resistance while being driven into the rock. The damaged threads appeared to have caused the nut to lock down before the collar on the wedge was fully engaged. It appears as though the collars were, however, partially engaged, which might have added to the illusion that the bolts were solid.

There are additional questions that need to be analyzed. The first of those should address the bolt installation. Was there added resistance with the bolt's installation? If this is true, how old was the drill bit and was the bit's diameter still acceptable enough to drill a quality hole? Was the bolt simply hammered too hard or too irregularly? What damaged the threads?

Second, we should address common practices with climbing. How many people lower off a single bolt when they cannot reach an anchor? Should there have been a back-up? Would a back-up have even been effective, what with the climber so close to the ground when the bolt failed? What are safer transitions when cleaning a sport climb?

Lastly, though a simple well-placed wedge anchor will often suffice in a roof placement in the dense Nuttall sandstone of the Meadow River Gorge, modern practices increasingly dictate other types of anchors, such as glue-ins, for such situations. (Source: Patrick Weaver, Appalachian Mountain Institute)

(Editor's Note: It is important to note that the bolt did not "fail". The analysis here is very thorough and will hopefully be distributed to the sport climbing community and read carefully.)

INTOXICATION – FALL ON ROCK, FREE SOLO CLIMBING
West Virginia, New River Gorge National River

In early July about 11:45 a.m., Charles G. Fredricks Jr. (39) fell while free solo climbing Angel's Arête (5.10) in the Bridge Buttress area. National Park Service rangers were on the scene within minutes and stabilized Fredricks using a backboard and placing him into a litter before transporting him. He was badly injured and suffered multi-system trauma from the fall.

Analysis

A witness to the fall reported that Fredricks had been drinking, and noted that he had consumed a fifth of vodka and at least three beers. (Source: Edited from a post on rockclimbing.com)

(Editor's Note: We have to include this in the data, but the primary cause has nothing to do with climbing.)

AVALANCHE, POOR POSITION, WEATHER, INEXPERIENCE
Wyoming, Cody South Fork, Deer Creek

On January 28, we were halfway down a steep 400-foot gully on our way to Deer Creek, where we would then walk downstream to the

Ghosts, a couple of WI 3+/4 routes that I had done ten years earlier. The gully is a popular alternative to the steeper, more involved approach that can be made downstream of the routes.

Ten years ago we made the steeper descent to the creek but walked out via the gully. On that day there were a few inches of dry snow on top of loose talus, and what had initially appeared to be the easy way out proved to be an exhausting, two-steps-forward, one-step-back slog to the trail above. My partner forgot his new gloves at the base of the routes and was so beat when we got to the trail that he decided they were not worth retrieving.

Remembering this, I opted for a rappel from a group of six or so medium-sized trees. It proved unnecessary, as the snow on the slope was knee-deep and well consolidated. I went first and after getting off rappel stepped to the side to avoid anything that might come rolling my way. There was a large fallen tree a few feet to my left that was held in place on the slope by three live trees that it had rolled up against. I coiled the ropes in a butterfly as my partner pulled them down.

Half of the first rope was on my shoulders when we heard a very loud noise in an otherwise mostly silent space. To me it was like a jet had just dropped down on top of us. My partner says, "Freight train!" It took a moment before we realized what was going on, and then the next thought I had was, "Where is it?" I looked to the top of the gully where blue sky was visible in the gap between the trees that line the sides of the chute. Almost immediately, sky was replaced by a burst of white shining powder snow. It looked as if somebody had set off a charge under the trail above.

I had previously witnessed only small slides, and at a comfortable distance. I knew some things about avalanches: what factors increase the hazard and what to do if you're caught in one. But I've never taken a class and had so little experience with them that my reaction to the slide was more instinctual than educated. A few quick steps to the left and we snugged up against the fallen tree. In the one or two seconds it took for us get into our positions, the slide was already on top of us.

My guess is that the event lasted some 30 – 90 seconds, but there's no way to know for sure. Crouched in complete darkness, a rumbling above me and feeling the vibration in the ground below, it seemed to take forever. I can remember thinking, "This should be over by now." But it just kept rumbling on. In the center of the slide's path there was a deep channel of dark clusters of rock glued together by wet snow. It kept moving for at least a full minute after the rest of the slide had stopped. Before it stopped, the half of the rope that I was coiling – which was not on my shoulders but still on the ground – got caught up in all of this debris and the rope started reeling off my neck. Luckily I had my left hand on a nub of a broken limb on the fallen tree, because eventually the rope snagged on itself and pulled me away from the log until my then outstretched arm kept me from being pulled further down the slope. Suddenly, the snow that had been flying over my back began to accumulate on top of it. It got very heavy very quickly and pressed me down until I got a mouthful of snow. At that moment I had the first conscious thought that I might be buried and die. It hadn't dawned on me before this that the slide might stop on top of me instead of passing over.

But then, there wasn't much conscious thought going on for most of the event; it was just pure experience, absent thought or emotion. Very shortly afterward, the slide stopped. There was maybe only a foot or so of snow on my back, and I stood up to find my partner and myself gratefully unharmed. The pile of debris at the bottom of the gully was roughly 20 feet deep and 100 feet across!

We went on to climb the Ghosts, and from the top of the routes we could see the dark, center part of the slide on the slope across the creek. Above the trail that we descended from there were a couple of wet spots on vertical rock with remnants of a frozen flow at their tops. It could be that one or both of these flows collapsed in the warm sun that afternoon, causing the slide. But there was also very much more snow than I had seen before in that drainage or in the South Fork as a whole. And it was a very warm and sunny day – forecast for 40's and likely closer to 50 degrees when the slide occurred at about two-thirty that afternoon.

Analysis

Considering both larger than normal overall accumulations of snow and recent large accumulations of snow, as well as the warm temperatures that day, I knew that there might be an elevated risk of avalanches. We maybe had some false comfort in the notion that the South Fork area is generally regarded to have a low risk for these events, and perhaps that's something that needs to change. One route, Smooth Emerald Milkshake – which is located in the Deer Creek drainage – is the only route that is noted in the guidebook as being particularly avalanche prone, and we weren't on it. On our way out we saw evidence of three other slides that started above, and then crossed over, the trail. Avalanches do happen in the Cody South Fork.

In retrospect, I am embarrassed to have ignored that the gully we were in was about 45 degrees—prime avalanche territory— and that it was a clear, treeless chute on an otherwise forested slope. In the pictures of our belay at the top of the gully, there are numerous very clear scars on the trees we anchored to that are roughly six or seven feet off the ground. I believe these were caused by passing debris.

Know the conditions that precipitate avalanches and be alert to your surroundings. Look for evidence of prior slides to identify common slide paths. Learn what to do if you are caught in a slide because they move very rapidly and you won't have time to think about it once you find yourself in harm's way. And do not let an area's reputation for low avalanche hazard blind you to the indicators of higher risk that are present. (Source: Jerry Wingenter – 49)

AVALANCHE, POOR POSITION
Wyoming, Grand Teton National Park, Meadows of Garnet Canyon

On April 18, Grand Teton National Park received a report of two overdue backcountry skiers who were in the park to ski the Grand Teton. The resulting search for the two men would eventually span seven days, encompass all of Garnet Canyon to include the North and South Forks, and would involve over 100 people. Though this large-scale search resulted in finding the two victims, it would ultimately show that both men died sometime Saturday night of April 16 while sleeping in their tent, victims of a very large avalanche.

Analysis

A truly tragic event claimed the lives of these two men as they slept in what they may have perceived as a safe camping spot. Or did they think that this was not as safe as it looked? We can only speculate on what they had been thinking at the time they erected their camp for the evening, but a few indications merit discussion.

Both men had received basic avalanche training early in their mountaineering careers and were considered experienced backcountry skiers and mountaineers by family, friends and acquaintances. They had received condition reports from a multitude of people as well as avalanche reports from the Bridger Teton Avalanche Center and the Grand Teton National Park Permits Station. All of these reports painted a bleak picture of what these men would encounter as they made their ascent.

We know that on April 16 at about 12:00 p.m. the two men had received a permit at the Moose Permits Desk to camp in the Meadows of Garnet Canyon. Later, between 3:00 and 6:00 p.m., the two skied through a camp in an area below the Platforms where they had brief interactions and conversations with the four skiers who were camped there. Based on the conversations, it appeared to the four that the two skiers had an original plan to ski the Grand Teton, but the impression was that their plan had been downgraded, though they did indicate they were thinking of travelling a little higher than the Meadows to take a look around. Discussions were also focused on the current poor weather and avalanche conditions. Based on the weather conditions on Saturday, low cloud cover, it was likely that they could not see very high into the canyon and may not have been able to see how high the north facing slope extended above their camp. When addressing the fact that they had left their avalanche beacons on, but were not wearing them, we are left to wonder if they had some indication during the night that they were closer to an avalanche prone area than they originally thought. The spot in which they were found is in a treeless area at the bottom of a large alluvial fan prone to avalanche activity. Most of the large boulders in that area are typically surrounded on one side by spin drifts that afford a good wind break and allow some people to camp in a wind sheltered spot near the base of the boulders, as these men had appeared to have noticed. One of the drifts on a nearby boulder was about five feet deep. These drifts would act like a bucket in the event of an avalanche reaching them.

A party of skiers reported that they had been through the lower Meadows area on Friday and had not seen any notable avalanche debris. In an interview with a local skier, he reported that as he was skiing through the lower Meadows on Monday morning, he observed a very large amount of avalanche deposition near the base of the North Face of Nez Perce. These observations would put the avalanche having occurred between Friday afternoon and Sunday night. Statements from the four skiers camped below the Platforms indicate they had heard several large avalanches on Saturday night.

Though evidence of the avalanche was buried less than 30 inches of new snowfall, there was a faint crown observed in a large bowl on the north side of Nez Perce Peak, approximately 1,200 feet above the campsite. If this slide initiated during Saturday night, it would have spilled over a 200 hundred-foot cliff and triggered another slide directly above the camp. These avalanches most likely swept down in waves, one right after the other.

The tent in which the two were sleeping had every indication that the avalanche that buried it did not sweep in but rather fell directly onto it. It was crushed from above. Based on their positions, both men were instantly buried under three-plus meters of snow, entombed inside their tent, unable to move. Most likely the sheer weight of the snow squeezed the breath from them and certainly did not allow them to take a breath in. They most likely blacked out quickly prior to suffocation.

Our sympathy goes out to the family and friends of these two adventurers as the local skiing and mountaineering community is left with another solemn reminder of the unwavering power of these mountains. (Source: Ranger Chris Harder – Incident Commander)

FALL ON SNOW/ICE
Wyoming, Grand Teton National Park, Teewinot

On June 4 about 0830, Jesse Stover (39) slipped and fell about 2,000 feet on the East Face route of Teewinot. He was ascending the peak with two other partners with the intent of skiing the East Face. He was at the crux of the East Face, the Narrows, around 11,600 feet when he slipped and fell, tumbling and cartwheeling until he came to rest at the level of the Apex (9,600 feet). He sustained severe injuries to his lower extremities, along with generalized trauma to the rest of his body. Another climber witnessed the fall and called Grand Teton National Park (GRTE) dispatch, which notified the rescue coordinator. GRTE SAR rangers were summoned along with Teton County Search and Rescue (TCSAR) volunteers. With two rangers on scene, and with the assistance of the TCSAR helicopter, J. Stover was short-hauled from the accident scene around 1145 to the Rescue Cache at Lupine Meadows and then transported to the hospital via GRTE ambulance.

Analysis

At 0400 J. Stover and partners (A. Japel and D. Stal) left the Lupine Meadows parking area to ascend and ski descend the East Face route of Teewinot Mountain. Conditions were ideal. Snow was firm with some boot penetration, which was great for ascending but too firm for skiing. Stover stated that he felt his crampon was balled-up with snow as he stepped into the six to eight-foot deep steep snow runnel. This may have provoked his fall. He was using an ice ax and snow whippet (ski pole with ice ax head) and both were firmly placed in the snow when he fell. However, the snow was unconsolidated below the placements and the force of his fall caused the tools to slip through the snow with no purchase whatsoever. When his feet hit the bottom of the runnel, the snow was rock-hard, and the sudden crampon purchase caused him to tumble, head over heels. Stover sustained severe injuries to his lower extremities, especially his left lower leg (open fracture, significant deformity, and uncontrollable bleeding), along with generalized trauma to the rest of his body. He was wearing a helmet. He was quoted as saying, "If I hadn't had a helmet on, I'd be dead.

All members of the Stover's party were very experienced, local skiers, each with more than 15 years of ski mountaineering. All had beacons, shovels, probes, and at least one ice ax. They all had skied on Teewinot Mountain before, but not from that high an elevation. They were undertaking an adventure that was well within their capabilities.

Teewinot is often underestimated by both novices and experienced mountaineers. During early season, the Narrows can present various (often unexpected) conditions. In this case, substantial steepness with hidden, unconsolidated snow on the sides of the runnel, with solid snow/ice conditions in the bottom of the runnel, proved disastrous. Crampons balling with snow as the day warmed augmented the possibility of a slip on snow, and the conditions of the runnel made self-arrest near impossible.

It is hard to fault the Stover party for the accident. They were well prepared and well within their capabilities. A rope could have made a difference, providing that it was well anchored and members were on belay. But anchoring the rope in their location could have been challenging and time-consuming. Had the rope not been well anchored, all members of the party conceivably could have fallen. Finally, most climbers/skiers with their agenda would be more concerned with moving through the mountains expeditiously and being off the mountains before avalanches commenced late morning/ early afternoon.

Stover stated that his party was having an incredibly enjoyable experience, and the slip and resulting tumble was completely unexpected. A beautiful day became a disaster in a split second. In my opinion, an unfortunate set of circumstances provoked this disaster. (Source: Ranger George Montopoli –Incident Commander)

FALL ON ROCK, ROPE JAMMED – SO SLACK IN ROPE, FAILURE TO FOLLOW INSTRUCTIONS
Wyoming, Grand Teton National Park, Guides Wall

In mid-June around 1400, Dagmar Rapp (47) was being guided up the Double Crack on guides Wall and was on the Flake Pitch. The guide had combined the last two pitches and was belaying from the top of the last pitch. The rope above Rapp had become jammed in a crack, so as she ascended, slack increased in the rope. The guide, feeling the rope tight, did not know the slack was developing and assumed Rapp was not moving. When Rapp was ten to 15 feet above the ledge she fell, landing on the ledge on her left flank. Another party informed the guide that she had an injured client. She lowered her second client to the ledge, and then belayed up a private (non-guided), good climber to her so that the pitch could be cleaned. The guide rappelled the normal descent route and walked back around the ledge to her clients

She then called park dispatch for assistance. SAR Coordinator James Springer received the call and paged out the Jenny Lake Rangers at 1445. Helicopter 25HX arrived at Lupine Meadows rescue cache at 1514. During this time rangers Vidak, Hays, and Armitage were directed to travel from their location at the base of Symmetry Spire to the start of technical climbing of Guides Wall. They arrived at the base of the wall at 1615.

Ranger Guenther was inserted by helicopter to the scene at 1620. Guenther evaluated the patient and determined she could be evacuated using the Screamer Suit. The patient and ranger Guenther were extracted from the ledge and landed on the ground at the Lupine Meadows Cache at 1705. Rapp was transported to St. Johns Hospital via park ambulance. (Source: Ranger Jim Springer – Incident Commander)
Analysis
Dagmar Rapp is an experienced climber who sometimes prefers to go with a guide. She was aware of the slack in the rope, but thought that she could complete the pitch without a mishap. She was not following the basic protocol of not climbing until the belay rope was snug. The guide's assumption that Rapp was not moving was logical. (Source: Jed Williamson)

FALL ON SNOW – SKI MOUNTAINEERING, UNABLE TO SELF-ARREST
Wyoming, Middle Teton, Ellingwood Couloir

At 0140 July 2, Ryan Redmond (32), Ben Johnson, Rob Backlund, and Kevin Salys departed the Lupine Meadows trailhead intending to climb and then ski the Ellingwood Couloir on the south side of the Middle Teton in Grand Teton National Park. After an uneventful approach to the bottom of the couloir, they began their ascent at dawn. Clear skies and cool nighttime temperatures created a firm, icy snow surface. The quartet used ice axes and crampons to facilitate their climb. Johnson and Salys climbed to the top of the couloir. About two thirds of the way up the couloir, Redmond and Backlund ended their ascent. Redmond was tired and they felt that because a runnel was in the middle of the couloir above them, the best skiing conditions would be in the lower section.

They donned their skis and at approximately 1000. Backlund watched Redmond begin his ski descent. He was surprised by how aggressively Redmond made his initial turns. Redmond made three telemark turns, then fell. He slid head downhill on his back. He was wearing a climbing helmet and had attached an ice ax to one of his ski poles. His attempts to arrest the fall were unsuccessful.

Reportedly, he screamed once. During the fall he went over a slight dip or bump in the couloir, which, according to Backlund, seemed to compress his body. He came to rest on an old avalanche debris cone at the mouth of the couloir and remained motionless. He fell approximately 800 vertical feet.

At 1010 Salys used his cell phone to contact a dispatcher at the Teton Interagency Dispatch Center. Salys said that he, Backlund, and Johnson were concerned about the snow conditions and that they would carefully descend to Redmond and assess his injuries. I mentioned that once they began their descent, cell phone coverage would be difficult. Though they tried several times to call during their descent, the initial call was the only direct contact I had with Salys, Johnson, or Backlund. Johnson was the first person to reach Redmond around 1130. Redmond was unconscious and his skis had come off. Other climbers in the area came to help. Johnson provided initial patient care. Backlund and Salys successfully down climbed the couloir joining Johnson and other rescuers at 1320.

At 1020 I contacted rangers Brian Hays and G.R. Fletcher. At 1220 they arrived at the scene of the accident. After they assessed Redmond's injuries, they suggested that a helicopter short-haul operation would provide the most efficient rescue. Redmond remained unconscious during the entire rescue.

Helicopter 20 HX arrived at Lupine Meadows at approximately 1230. At 1401 Redmond and Armitage were short-hauled from the bottom of the Ellingwood Couloir to the rescue cache. Dr. Will Smith, who serves as the Grand Teton National Park medical director, and several EMS providers stabilized his injuries and prepared him for the life flight. At 1441 Redmond left Lupine Meadows aboard an Air Idaho life flight, which took him to Eastern Idaho Regional Medical Center in Idaho Falls, where he was admitted in critical condition.

Fletcher, Hays, Backlund, Johnson, and Salys safely descended to the Lupine Meadows Trailhead and arrived at the rescue cache at 1900.

Analysis

Redmond is an AmeriCorps volunteer affiliated with the Teton Science School in Kelly, WY. Johnson and Backlund work for the

Teton Science School and Salys works for another organization in Wilson, WY. Johnson and Backlund were casually acquainted with Redmond through the Teton Science School. They had known each other for about a month. Johnson, Backlund, and Salys were better acquainted with each other and had embarked on previous ski mountaineering outings including some in the Teton Range. This was the first ski mountaineering trip either of them had taken with Redmond. Johnson and Backlund knew Redmond was a good skier. Conversations they had with Redmond indicated that he had been a high school ski racer and had some backcountry skiing experience. They weren't sure about his ski mountaineering background.

In discussing this accident with Backlund, Johnson, and Salys they offered these observations. They stated it would have been nice to know more about Redmond, including his emergency contact information and his ski mountaineering background. Backlund observed that Redmond had stated that he was excited to ski the Ellingwood Couloir and hoped to "ski it hard." This statement and the aggressive way Redmond initiated his turns surprised Backlund, who was more accustomed to a conservative approach of testing the snow with skis on before committing to more aggressive turns. Finally, they commented that it would be difficult to arrest a fall on the steep, firm snow that existed in the Ellingwood Couloir. This is an important point. On steep, firm snow a fall must be arrested immediately to avoid serious consequences. (Source: Ranger Ron Johnson – Incident Commander)

OFF ROUTE, FALL ON SNOW/ICE – UNABLE TO SELF-ARREST, FAULTY USE OF CRAMPONS, NO HARD HAT, INEXPERIENCE
Wyoming, Grand Teton National Park, Middle Teton

About 1000 on July 29, Ryan Haymaker (21) and Andy Friedlund were attempting to climb the Middle Teton, but they mistakenly ascended the Ellingwood Couloir instead of the traditional Southwest Couloir farther to the west. Near the top of the Ellingwood Couloir they were unable to continue because the climbing became much steeper and significantly more difficult. They then began descending. Initially they down-climbed, but after a while they began to glissade with Friedlund going first. After descending about one-third of the couloir, Haymaker lost control and slid past Friedlund. He hit rock and began to tumble. He came to rest about 1,200 feet later on the apron just short of the talus. He sustained critical injuries.

Exum guide Chris Figenshau and Teton County SAR volunteer notified GTNP dispatch of the accident at 1043 and nearby climbers stabilized Haymaker. Four rangers were then shuttled by a GTNP contract helicopter to the incident scene. Once on scene, rangers further stabilized Haymaker, securing him onto a backboard. He was carried about 75 yards on the backboard to the helicopter, where he was loaded internally and flown to the Lupine Meadows Rescue Cache. Park Medical Advisor Dr. Will Smith provided advanced medical interventions. Haymaker was then transported to the Eastern Idaho Regional Medical Center via their emergency helicopter. Haymaker's climbing partner, Andy Friedlund (21), was flown in helicopter to Lupine Meadows from the accident scene with the remaining three rangers.

Analysis

Ryan Haymaker had very little, if any, mountaineering experience. He was originally part of a group of four people who obtained the overnight permit for Garnet Canyon. They split into two parties in the canyon on their approach day. The following day, one party headed for the South Teton, and the other party (R. Haymaker and A. Friedlund) headed for Middle Teton. Because Haymaker and Friedlund headed up the wrong couloir, there is a good chance that they did not receive any information about the route at the Jenny Lake Ranger Station prior to the ascent. Those without prior knowledge often mistake the Ellingwood Couloir for the Southwest Couloir. It a very steep couloir approaching 50 degrees near its top and has a slant to it so that people who fall often crash into exposed rocks on its west side and middle. A sliding fall in the couloir without wearing helmet can be disastrous, as was the case with Haymaker. Furthermore, few experienced climbers would consider glissading this couloir wearing crampons. Most down-climb the couloir, and some even rappel it, creating anchors in the snow or on the rock walls on its sides. (Source: Ranger George Montopoli – Incident Commander)

FALL ON ROCK, CLIMBING ALONE, INEXPERIENCE
Wyoming, Grand Teton National Park, Grand Teton

On Saturday July 31, Don Ivie (44) arrived in Jackson with his wife Yvette from Springfield, Missouri. That afternoon, Ivie visited the Jenny Lake Ranger Station to inquire about route conditions and any other route information he could gather. During his contact with Ranger Schuster, he mentioned that he was going to start his climb at about 4:00 a.m. the following morning. Schuster advised him that it would probably be better for him to leave sometime around 1:00 a.m. in order to avoid potential afternoon storms. Schuster also advised Ivie that he would need an ice ax in order to get up and down from the Lower Saddle.

Later in the day, Ivie had a conversation with Ken Jern about climbing the Grand Teton the following day. Jern, a former Exum Mountain Guide with many years of experience climbing the Grand Teton, advised Ivie to take his time and, since Ivie was going to be in the area for nine days, become acclimatized to the elevation while attempting a smaller objective. Jern also suggested that Ivie should consider hiring a guide to take him up the Grand Teton. It appeared to Jern that Ivie was very determined that he was going to climb the Grand Teton early in the trip.

At 11:45 a.m. on Sunday, Ivie was left at the Lupine Meadows Trailhead by his wife Yvette as he set out for his climb. He was equipped with: a brown Camelback pack, a headlamp, a rented ice ax and crampons, a set of trekking poles, a climbing harness, some food bars, his cellular phone, a lightweight jacket, and a can of Red Bull. Yvette would not hear from Ivie until he text messaged her at about 9:40 a.m. from somewhere just above the Lower Saddle, stating that he was running a little later than planned so she should bump his pickup time back from 5:00 p.m. to 7:00 p.m. In the message, Ivie also included a photo of a Red Bull can resting on an area of black rock.

Sometime around 12:00 p.m., an Exum guide and his party were descending the Owen-Spalding route below the main rappel when they saw a lone man fitting Ivie's description resting on a rock. During the guide's brief interaction with him, the guide learned he was heading toward the Owen-Spalding climb for a solo ascent. The guide also noticed that he was wearing dark colored or brown lightweight hiking boots that looked to be of some unknown brand and seemed inappropriate for climbing the Grand Teton.

About 3:00 p.m., another climbing party noted that there was a brown Camelback lying near their packs close to the bottom of the main Owen-Spalding rappel. The pack looked like it was laid there with the intention of returning to it. This climbing party did not see any other individuals along the upper Owen-Spalding route from the summit other than the guided Exum party.

At 8:55 p.m. on July 31, I was contacted by Yvette Ivie concerning the whereabouts of her husband, Don, who was overdue from his climb

Analysis

We know that Don Ivie fell from somewhere along the beginning of the Owen-Spalding route on Sunday, July 31st after 12:00 p.m. Because this was an un-witnessed event, we may never know what exactly happened to cause his fall. However, there are a few factors that do seem to lead one to focus on his lack of overall ability to accomplish the task he set out upon.

Don Ivie was not an experienced mountaineer, nor did he posses any technical climbing experience that would have aided in both his climbing technique and route finding abilities. Prior to this trip, he had climbed once or twice at an indoor climbing gym on a route that he felt was equivalent to the difficulty he would encounter on the Grand Teton. While the Owen-Spalding route is rated fairly low on the difficulty scale, it is very exposed and, at certain points, awkward climbing especially for a beginner climber. The route finding is not straightforward and, for an inexperienced climber, complex. It is not unusual for climbers to get off-route and find themselves in an area far more difficult than their level of ability. Ivie's climbing experience and technique would have made the climb much more difficult than its rating suggests.

Another scenario that many beginner climbers do not take into account involves backing off or down-climbing a route. Though descending along the Crawl or Belly Roll may not be too much more difficult than ascending it, descending the Double Chimney, either from the top, or part way through the climb, would be very awkward and difficult. Though it's considered a relatively easy route, a mistake made along any portion of this climb while unroped will have dire consequences. It should also be noted that this route rarely sees solo ascents from climbers who have not already climbed it roped.

To climb the Grand Teton in one day is an undertaking not to be taken lightly. It is typically only accomplished by very fit individuals who are acclimatized and know the route well. At altitudes greater than 10,000 feet, rational decisions can be more difficult to make. Ivie lived at an altitude of about 1,300 feet. He had arrived in the Jackson Hole area less than 24 hours prior to the start of his climb.

Ivie's footwear was not adequate for a climb of this nature, nor was it designed for climbing on rock. With this type of hiking boot, a slip on the rock would not be uncommon and would make vertical climbing much more challenging.

Though the Owen-Spalding route was free of snow, recent rain storms had passed through the area so, since this part of the climb is not in the sun until late in the day, it is not unusual for small patches of ice, Vergas or black ice to develop in shady portions of the climb. Slipping on ice anywhere along the route would also contribute to a fall.

The most likely factors to contribute to this tragic outcome were the combination of poor judgment and inexperience compounded by the lack of appropriate equipment to safely ascend this route. Ivie's strong desire to have a successful attempt on the Grand Teton early in his trip appears to have swayed his sense of reasoning and pushed him well beyond his abilities. This was not simply a case of someone attempting a climb unseen and unknown. It is apparent that Ivie decided to ignore the advice he was given from a variety of experienced people.

All this having been said, we express our heartfelt condolences to the family, friends, and co-workers of this fallen adventurer. (Source: Ranger Chris Harder – Incident Commander)

LOOSE BLOCK PULLED OFF – FALL ON ROCK
Wyoming, Grand Teton National Park, Middle Teton

On August 9, a party of three was intending to climb the Buckingham Ridge on the Middle Teton. They were ascending the fourth-class approach slabs, unroped, when Steven Zalesky (43) pulled a large loose block off and fell about ten feet to a ledge and then tumbled an additional 60 feet. Zaleski's partners, M. Sohasky and D. Hemken, were out of sight of Zalesky when they heard rockfall. They shouted to Zalesky to see if he was injured, and Zalesky responded that he was "alive, but hurt".

They quickly down-climbed to his location and assessed his condition.

The loose block had grazed the right side of his head and shoulder, and his left ankle was probably injured when he hit the ledge. He was unable to walk after the accident. The most experienced climber, D. Hempken, descended the adjacent Ellingwood Couloir to the South Fork of Garnet Canyon to get better cell phone reception. M. Sohasky was eventually able to get cell phone reception from the accident site and made the initial call to TIDC.

Ranger Vidak requested a helicopter from the Teton Heli-base. After scouting the accident site, Heli 25 dropped rangers Springer and Edmonds at a landing zone in the South Fork of Garnet Canyon. Rangers Springer and Edmonds began climbing to the accident site (11,150 feet elevation) and arrived there at 1112.

Zalesky did not lose consciousness and was alert and oriented. Because of significant rockfall danger in the immediate area, it was decided to "Screamer Suit" the two climbers from the scene, with a ranger attending each climber. At 1158 Heli 20 departed 701 to extract Edmonds and Zalesky from the accident site. Attached to the short-haul line was a second Screamer Suit for Springer and the uninjured climber (Sohasky) to use for their extraction. At about 1200, Edmonds and the patient were extracted from the accident site and delivered to the rangers in the Garnet Canyon. Springer and the Sohasky were extracted from the scene at about 1215 and were delivered to the same LZ. Two more helicopter flights delivered Zalesky, Edmonds, Johnson, Springer, and Tyson to the cache by 1343. Sohasky and Hempken hiked out to the Lupine Meadows Trailhead.

Analysis

D. Hemken had 30 years of climbing experience and M. Sohasky had over eight years of experience. They had done several routes in the Tetons. The Buckingham Ridge (III 5.7) was well within their ability level. Steven Zalesky was the least experienced of the three, but had done a few routes in the Tetons and at least one (Jensen Ridge on Symmetry Spire) that was comparable in difficulty to the Buckingham.

The climbing party was doing everything right: they left their camp in the Garnet Meadows by 5:30 a.m., they were wearing helmets and rock shoes on the rock approach to the Buckingham Ridge, and they were on-route. The approach to the climb is mainly scrambling and is normally done un-roped, if one uses good route finding.

Most, if not all, of the mountaineering and rock routes on the higher peaks in the Teton Range have their share of loose rock, and one must be very careful when choosing hand and foot holds. Many very skilled climbers have had accidents involving loose rock, and one must be diligent in climbing through third and fourth-class terrain. (Source: Ranger Martin Vidak – Incident Commander)

FALL ON SNOW – LOSS OF CONTROL ON GLISSADE, INEXPERIENCE
Wyoming, Grand Teton National Park, Nez Perce

On August 11 between 1100 and 1600, Grand Teton National Park rangers and Teton Interagency Heli-tack personnel performed a 1,200-foot technical snow-lowering operation on the north side of Nez Perce Peak to rescue Laura Mason (21), who had fallen about 100 feet and suffered injuries to her left lower leg. She was glissading a snowfield to the west of the Hourglass Couloir. She was unable to control her speed and crashed into the rocks at the base of the snowfield.

Mason had been with her boyfriend, John Foss, and brother. They thought they were ascending Middle Teton, but were actually ascending Nez Perce. They decided that they needed to glissade down a snowfield some 100 feet to talus below in order to traverse to a better ascent line. In order to keep her pants from getting wet, Mason decided to wrap a garbage bag around her legs and buttocks. The snowfield was between 45 and 50 degrees and contained very firm snow that was icy in spots. She had an ice ax, but no crampons or helmet. She immediately lost control when she started to glissade. While Mason's boyfriend stayed with her, her brother ran down to the Garnet Canyon Meadows where he encountered rangers G.R. Fletcher and B. Hays.

At the accident location, Mason was medically stabilized, administered medications, and secured to a rescue litter. She was carried through talus a short distance, and then lowered about 1,200 feet on snow to the Cave Couloir landing zone. From there, Mason was placed inside the helicopter for a flight to the Lupine Meadows rescue cache, arriving about 1540. She was met by a park ambulance and transported to St. John's Medical Center in Jackson for further treatment.

Analysis

In addition to their inexperience and being on the wrong mountain on a questionable route, Laura Mason was extremely fortunate that she only fractured a leg, especially given the fact that she was not wearing a helmet.

The thoughtful dynamics of the SAR team (including the helicopter pilot) was evidenced by their ability to curtail the short-haul operation when the safety of the operation was compromised by environmental conditions. The ground-based operation took longer, but all returned home safely. No one was so focused on an expeditious short-haul that it obscured good judgment. To maintain a margin of safety, a SAR operation must evolve according to the conditions that are constantly presented. (Source: Ranger George Montopoli – Incident Commander)

FALL ON ROCK – LASS OF CONTROL ON BELAY, INEXPERIENCE, HASTE
Wyoming, Grand Teton national Park, Death Canyon

The climbing party of M. Ybarra, L. McLean, and Dana Reis left the Whitegrass Trailhead at 0900 on the morning of August 20 to climb the Snaz in Death Canyon. The Snaz is rated Grade IV, 5.9, and a few of the pitches offer 5.10 variations. From the top of the climb, one can either scramble off on 4th Class terrain or rappel the route.

The last pitch of is rated 5.7 and has a 5.10 + variation to the climber's right called "Cousin Leroy's Uncle". Ybarra chose this. He led it and then began belaying Reis and then McLean. These two were climbing on a "staggered belay" and were being belayed simultaneously with a Black Diamond Guide ATC.

Reis, climbing second, removed the protection that Ybarra had placed on lead. According to McLean, Reis was having difficulty climbing the pitch and was using the line belaying McLean to grab onto to assist herself over the difficult roof. In addition, McLean stated that she stopped climbing and hung on her rope when she saw Reis having difficulties. Because of the overhanging rock, McLean was unable to get back on the rock to continue climbing. McLean asked Ybarra to lower her so that she could get on a less overhanging section and once again begin climbing.

Ybarra stated to Ranger Martin Vidak that he was trying to "release the rope" from the belay device when the rope "shot out" and he lost control of the lower. The result was that McLean impacted a ledge with a fall of approximately 20 feet, injuring her left leg. She was unable to move, and Ybarra rappelled to her to assess her injuries. Before rappelling, Ybarra was able to make cell phone contact through the Teton Interagency Dispatch Center.

At 2035 Helicopter 25 left Whitegrass Ranch for the accident site. At 2043 Heli 25 extracted Ranger Baerwald and the patient from the scene, landing at Whitegrass Ranch at 2050.

Analysis

M. Ybarra had about six years of climbing experience and had climbed many multi-pitch routes in the mountains. D. Reis and L. McLean were experienced indoor climbers and had led some sport climbs, but had little or no experience in climbing multi-pitch routes in a mountain environment. The three climbers met earlier in the summer at Smith Rocks and made plans to climb in the Tetons in August.

The three climbed Irene's Arête (III, 5.8) a few days prior to their Snaz climb. It is worth noting that the Snaz, in particular the Cousin Leroy's Uncle variation (5.10+), is significantly harder than Irene's Arête.

The party left the Whitegrass Trailhead at about 0900, which is a fairly late start for a party of three on a Grade IV climb, especially considering that two of the three had no experience with multi-pitch climbs. The approach to the Snaz takes most parties about two hours.

According to Ybarra, he saw approaching thunderstorms and lightning and "was in a rush" at the time of the accident. They carried no packs and had no water on the climb itself. They were planning on doing the 4th Class walk-off to descend, then decided to rappel the route when they noticed fixed anchors.

If the second climber, D. Reis, had not cleaned the protection after she climbed the pitch, it is likely that L. McLean would not have swung off the rock, which then required a lower. It is good practice for the second climber to leave gear in and "back-clip" it into the rope belaying the third climber on a traversing pitch.

The Black Diamond "Guide ATC" device is commonly used to belay two climbers at once. However, a good understanding of its use and limitations is necessary for both the belayer and the seconding climbers. When the belayer is lowering a climber whose weight is on the rope, he must be well versed in this procedure so as not to lose control of the lower, which is what happened here. It is prudent to practice this technique before having to use it in a real situation. (Source: Ranger Martin Vidak – Incident Commander)

FALL ON SNOW – UNABLE TO SELF-ARREST, FAULTY USE OF CRAMPONS
Wyoming, Gannet Peak

On August 10 about 1300, the Sublette County Sheriff's dispatch center received a call from a party of five on the summit ridge of Gannet Peak (13,804 feet). The party stated that one of the members of their group had lost his footing and had fallen, then slid down the east face snowcap, just near the summit of Gannet. They said he had lost his ice ax (failed to self arrest) and had slid out of their line of sight towards the large cliff band that separates the upper peak and the Gooseneck Glacier. The snowcap on Gannet peak is very steep near the summit and gets steeper and steeper towards the cliff band. The reporting party was not able to get to the fallen member because of this terrain and could not tell what condition he may be in.

Tip Top Search and Rescue of Sublette County was paged out and responded in their contract helicopter (Bell L4). Members Milford Lockwood, Jason Ray, and Tony Chambers along with pilot John Ruhl departed the Pinedale airport at 1424. Sublette County emergency management coordinator Jim Mitchell and Tip Top member Leanne Rellstab manned an incident command post to monitor the operation.

Upon arrival at the scene, the rescue crew was able to quickly identify the reporting party located just below the summit ridge and then the slide path of the missing subject. After a quick aerial search, the subject – Don Scott (63) of was located in the rocks just below the snowcap, but fortunately above the cliff band and Gooseneck Glacier. He had slid roughly 350 vertical feet. Scott appeared to be unresponsive to the helicopter crew but his exact condition was at this point unknown.

The rescue crew, in conjunction with the incident command post, decided that the quickest and safest way to access the climber was to use the short-haul method. The rescue crew established a landing zone in the Dinwoody drainage at 10,800 feet, rigged for short haul, performed a check flight, and satisfied all other safety parameters. The crew inserted one short-hauler to the accident scene and at 1545 determined that Scott was deceased.

Gannet Peak's summit ridge is the divide between Fremont and Sublette County. Since the climber had fallen into the Fremont County side, the mission was a joint effort between Fremont County and Sublette County. At this point the Fremont County coroner requested that the rescue crew fly to Lander, allowing Fremont County officials to determine the safest way to remove the body. The Fremont County coroner requested that the Sublette County crew remove the body using the short haul method. A recovery attempt was made the following morning, but for two consecutive days high winds prevented all attempts. The following morning (August 13) conditions were favorable, and a successful body recovery was made.

Analysis

The climbing party of five was moderately experienced. In the past, as a group, they completed climbing trips together at least on an annual basis, but not on a regular basis. Failure to self-arrest by the subject was obviously the biggest error made that day. The subject was also wearing crampons, which may have contributed to his fall. When Scott was located, it was apparent that he had also lost his helmet. (It was found one crack system to the north). Over the years, I have often times noticed just how many people wear their helmets loosely or improperly. I have no idea if this was the case with Mr. Scott, but since his helmet did come off, I have wondered if it was secure. (Source: Tony Chambers, Tip Top Search and Rescue)

AVALANCHE – FAILURE TO ANALYZE SNOWPACK, POOR POSITION
Wyoming, Snowy Range

On November 6th, Brice Portwood (27) and I (Ed Warren – 25) were trying to climb a mixed route (a summer rock route, but never climbed as a mixed/ice climb as far as we know) in the Snowy Range. Conditions were not ideal at 0800 when we left the car, with winds between 15 and 25 mph and occasionally higher gusts and temps in the low teens. But the sky was clear at the trailhead with clouds around the peak, and the forecast for the rest of the day was improving conditions. It was a pretty typical WY winter day.

Snowpack was unusually low. Typically, by November, the highway department closes Route 130, but because of the abnormally scarce snowfall, it was still open. The approach to the climb was a quick two miles with snowpack never more than knee deep. At the base of the climb, we discovered deeper snow. We dug a snow pit (doubling as a belay platform) and didn't notice any layering or slabs.

Brice led the first pitch, which was mostly mixed terrain. I led the second pitch, which was almost exclusively ice, and found a spot to belay underneath a slight protrusion of rock on the right side that I hoped might provide a bit of protection from falling ice.

We were a good 400+ feet up, having stretched-out the first two pitches. Brice led the third pitch. When he was about 100 feet above me, he reached the top of the ice slot and encountered a snow band. He shouted down that the terrain had moderated and it would be a ways to the next potential anchor so we might have to simul-climb again for a bit. I told him I understood.

Brice proceeded to try to make his way through the snow that lay above. He described it as thigh deep but that it felt deeper due to the angle. He tried to get out of the snow band by climbing some exposed rock, but it wouldn't go, so he returned to the snow. He had placed two pieces of protection to that point, a screw in the ice slot and a #6 BD stopper in the rock that was exposed higher up.

At that point (about 20-30 minutes after Brice first entered the snow band), I disconnected myself from the anchor because there was little rope left and the plan was to simul-climb. Only minutes after disconnecting myself, the snowpack around Brice failed under his weight and it began sliding. It slid 200 feet, carrying Brice and funneling into the slot where I was perched. The only thing I noticed was the snowy rope sliding towards me. I looked up and saw a wall of snow about to hit me. The next thing I knew I was upside and backwards being shoved down the climb beneath the falling snow. I thought I fell for much farther than I actually did, because once the rope stopped me, the snow continued to fall over me, giving the sensation of movement.

When the snow finally fell past me, I was hanging upside down. If I remember correctly, there was one half rope holding me taught by my harnesses. This rope had complete sheath failure and was exposing three feet of core. The other half rope was caught around the boot and displaced crampon of my shattered ankle. Both ropes were holding at least part of my body weight. It took about five minutes to extricate myself from the tangle around my left ankle, while hanging upside down. During this time, Brice, who had come to a stop unharmed about 60 feet above me, ensured I was all right and then began down climbing towards me.

Once I extricated myself, I put two ice screws into the pitch and attached myself, although at that point I realized how dangerous it was to be attached directly to the ice without the rope acting as a key dynamic element – which had saved me the first time—in the event that any more snow broke loose.

It took two rappels to get down. Brice did each one first so that he could set up the next rappel station and get things ready at the base of the climb. The first rappel was trickier, and Brice held the ends of the rope so that he could arrest my fall if I lost control. The second rappel was more straightforward, and I was feeling quite capable despite the pain.

Once at the base of the climb, I began scooting on my butt down the moderate slope. At the bottom, I tried hopping on my right leg (laceration and partial quad tendon tear) while holding onto Brice, but I quickly realized it wouldn't work due to the snowdrifts and weak 'good' leg. Brice suggested carrying me using a rope backpack, but it didn't seem feasible to me, considering I outweighed him by 20 pounds and I was sure the soft snow would cause us to fall over repeatedly. So we rigged a dragging setup. We used my backpack as a sled, with me attached directly to it by my harness and a tether for Brice to pull on.

With me pushing with my arms and the help of the slight downhill slope, we made decent but exhausting progress. Once the terrain leveled out, though, our progress came to a quick stop. At this point, the only option was for me to crawl under my own power. Brice went ahead, packing down the snow, and I followed. We did this for the last mile and a half until we got back to the car.

Analysis

In my calculus, we made two major errors. First, we failed to anticipate the likelihood of an avalanche in any substantial way before we started our climb. I didn't take the time to even consider it as a serious risk. Second, and more importantly, once we encountered deep snow high on the climb, we failed again to recognize the risk. Compounding this was the nature of the terrain. Because I was belaying from a slot, any sliding snow above would find its way to me and I would have no place to hide. Snow bands across couloirs are a common feature in alpine climbing and that caused us to be complacent. In addition, I rationalized that our slot was not oriented in such a way that it would funnel the snow above. However, we should have recognized these basic ingredients in what turned out to be a recipe for disaster: questionable snowpack above a constricted route. Upon finding the snow-loaded slope above our climb, we should have turned around and called it a day. (Source: Ed Warren)

(Editor's Note: This team videoed much of this event. It can be found on YouTube. We thank them for this candid report.)

STATISTICAL TABLES

TABLE I
REPORTED MOUNTAINEERING ACCIDENTS

	Number of Accidents Reported		Total Persons Involved		Injured		Fatalities	
	USA	CAN	USA	CAN	USA	CAN	USA	CAN
1951	15		22		11		3	
1952	31		35		17		13	
1953	24		27		12		12	
1954	31		41		31		8	
1955	34		39		28		6	
1956	46		72		54		13	
1957	45		53		28		18	
1958	32		39		23		11	
1959	42	2	56	2	31	0	19	2
1960	47	4	64	12	37	8	19	4
1961	49	9	61	14	45	10	14	4
1962	71	1	90	1	64	0	19	1
1963	68	11	79	12	47	10	19	2
1964	53	11	65	16	44	10	14	3
1965	72	0	90	0	59	0	21	0
1966	67	7	80	9	52	6	16	3
1967	74	10	110	14	63	7	33	5
1968	70	13	87	19	43	12	27	5
1969	94	11	125	17	66	9	29	2
1970	129	11	174	11	88	5	15	5
1971	110	17	138	29	76	11	31	7
1972	141	29	184	42	98	17	49	13
1973	108	6	131	6	85	4	36	2
1974	96	7	177	50	75	1	26	5
1975	78	7	158	22	66	8	19	2
1976	137	16	303	31	210	9	53	6
1977	121	30	277	49	106	21	32	11
1978	118	17	221	19	85	6	42	10
1979	100	36	137	54	83	17	40	19
1980	191	29	295	85	124	26	33	8
1981	97	43	223	119	80	39	39	6
1982	140	48	305	126	120	43	24	14
1983	187	29	442	76	169	26	37	7
1984	182	26	459	63	174	15	26	6

	Number of Accidents Reported		Total Persons Involved		Injured		Fatalities	
	USA	CAN	USA	CAN	USA	CAN	USA	CAN
1985	195	27	403	62	190	22	17	3
1986	203	31	406	80	182	25	37	14
1987	192	25	377	79	140	23	32	9
1988	156	18	288	44	155	18	24	4
1989	141	18	272	36	124	11	17	9
1990	136	25	245	50	125	24	24	4
1991	169	20	302	66	147	11	18	6
1992	175	17	351	45	144	11	43	6
1993	132	27	274	50	121	17	21	1
1994	158	25	335	58	131	25	27	5
1995	168	24	353	50	134	18	37	7
1996	139	28	261	59	100	16	31	6
1997	158	35	323	87	148	24	31	13
1998	138	24	281	55	138	18	20	1
1999	123	29	248	69	91	20	17	10
2000	150	23	301	36	121	23	24	7
2001	150	22	276	47	138	14	16	2
2002	139	27	295	29	105	23	34	6
2003	118	29	231	32	105	22	18	6
2004	160	35	311	30	140	16	35	14
2005	111	19	176	41	85	14	34	7
2006	109		227		89		21	
2007	113		211		95		15	
2008	112		203		96		19	
2009	126		240		112		23	
2010	185		389		151		34	
2011	156		346		109		28	
Totals:	6,912	958	12,782	2003	5,810	715	1,513	292

TABLE II

Geographical Districts	1951–2010			2011		
	Number of Accidents	Deaths	Total Persons Involved	Number of Accidents	Deaths	Total Persons Involved
Canada[N.B.]						
Alberta	520	142	1033			
British Columbia	317	119	641			
Yukon Territory	37	28	77			
New Brunswick	1	0	0			
Ontario	37	9	67			
Quebec	31	10	63			
East Arctic	8	2	21			
West Arctic	2	2	2			
Practice Cliffs[1]	20	2	36			
United States						
Alaska	555	201	946	15	9	40
Arizona, Nevada, Texas	100	18	185	6	0	11
Atlantic–North	1047	151	1801	13	0	23
Atlantic–South	143	33	257	26	2	50
California	1382	302	724	24	3	38
Central	136	18	219	1	0	6
Colorado	841	229	2465	31	0	59
Montana, Idaho South Dakota	90	35	148	0	0	0
Oregon	218	116	486	6	3	23
Utah, New Mex.	184	60	337	3	1	6
Washington	1074	328	972	18	6	53
Wyoming	588	140	1079	13	4	37

[N.B.] No data from 2006-2011

[1] This category includes bouldering, artificial climbing walls, buildings, and so forth. These are also added to the count of each province, but not to the total count, though that error has been made in previous years. The Practice Cliffs category has been removed from the U.S. data.

TABLE III   STATISTICAL TABLES /121

	1951–10 USA	1959–04 CAN.	2011 USA	2011 CAN.
Terrain				
Rock	4735	528	103	
Snow	2461	355	49	
Ice	282	15	4	
River	15	3	0	
Unknown	22	10	0	
Ascent or Descent				
Ascent	3790	587	104	
Descent	1123	371	49	
Unknown	256	13	1	
Other [N.B.]	12	0	2	
Immediate Cause				
Fall or slip on rock	3745	290	83	
Slip on snow or ice	1071	207	23	
Falling rock, ice, or object	653	137	6	
Exceeding abilities	557	32	7	
Illness [1]	420	26	17	
Stranded	368	53	8	
Avalanche	304	127	8	
Rappel Failure/Error [2]	315	47	12	
Exposure	278	14	1	
Loss of control/glissade	215	17	9	
Nut/chock pulled out	254	9	7	
Failure to follow route	219	30	7	
Fall into crevasse/moat	169	50	5	
Faulty use of crampons	115	6	3	
Piton/ice screw pulled out	95	13	0	
Ascending too fast	72	0	1	
Skiing [3]	64	11	2	
Lightning	47	7	0	
Equipment failure	16	3	0	
Other [4]	549	37	24	
Unknown	61	10	0	
Contributory Causes				
Climbing unroped	1031	165	10	
Exceeding abilities	955	202	20	
Placed no/inadequate protection	813	96	17	
Inadequate equipment/clothing	717	70	7	

	1951–10 USA	1959–04 CAN.	2011 USA	2011 CAN.
Weather	495	67	16	
Climbing alone	420	69	6	
No hard hat	359	71	4	
Inadequate belay [2]	249	28	4	
Nut/chock pulled out	209	32	6	
Poor position	211	20	4	
Darkness	165	21	3	
Party separated	118	12	6	
Failure to test holds	105	32	3	
Piton/ice screw pulled out	86	13	0	
Failed to follow directions	70	12	0	
Exposure	65	16	1	
Illness[1]	40	9	0	
Equipment failure	13	7	0	
Other[4]	282	100	17	
Age of Individuals				
Under 15	1247	12	0	
15-20	1307	203	7	
21-25	1455	257	25	
26-30	1373	211	28	
31-35	2057	114	25	
36-50	1374	143	46	
Over 50	323	31	13	
Unknown	2070	530	27	
Experience Level				
None/Little	1852	304	20	
Moderate (1 to 3 years)	1677	354	27	
Experienced	2173	440	69	
Unknown	2249	559	56	
Month of Year				
January	245	25	5	
February	222	55	2	
March	336	68	10	
April	431	39	11	
May	961	62	16	
June	1153	70	29	
July	1199	254	24	
August	1107	184	23	
September	1199	75	12	
October	480	42	9	